QUIET TALKS WITH WORLD WINNERS

S. D. GORDON'S
QUIET TALKS

Quiet Talks on Power
Quiet Talks on Prayer
Quiet Talks on Service

Quiet Talks About Jesus
Quiet Talks on Personal Problems
Quiet Talks with World Winners

Quiet Talks About the Tempter
Quiet Talks on Home Ideals
Quiet Talks About Our Lord's Return

Quiet Talks on Following the Christ
Quiet Talks About the Crowned Christ of the Revelation
Quiet Talks on John's Gospel

BOOKLETS

A Quiet Talk with Those Who Weep.
A Quiet Talk about the Babe of Bethlehem
Prayer Changes Things
The Consummation of Calvary
Crowding Out the Christ Child
Keeping Tryst. Decorated boards,
Jesus Habits of Prayer. Decorated boards
The Quietest Talk. 16mo, paper
The Quiet Time. With Daily Prayer Pages.

Quiet Talks with World Winners

BY

S. D. GORDON

Author of "Quiet Talks on Power," "Quiet Talks About Jesus," "Quiet Talks on Personal Problems," Etc.

NEW YORK   CHICAGO   TORONTO
FLEMING H. REVELL COMPANY
LONDON AND EDINBURGH

Copyright, 1908, by
A. C. ARMSTRONG & SON

Copyright transferred, 1910, to
FLEMING H. REVELL CO.

New York: 158 Fifth Avenue
Chicago: 17 North Wabash Ave.
London: 21 Paternoster Square
Edinburgh: 75 Princes Street

CONTENTS

I. WORLD-WINNING.

                                                                              PAGE

1. The Master Passion 7
2. The Master's Plan 35
3. The Need 59
4. The Present Opportunity 81
5. The Pressing Emergency 103
6. The Past Failure 119
7. The Coming Victory 133

II. WINNING FORCES.

1. The Church 153
2. Each One of Us 169
3. Jesus 189
4. The Holy Spirit 205
5. Prayer 225
6. Money 245
7 Sacrifice 263

THE MASTER PASSION

The Earliest Calvary Picture.
The Love Passion.
Mother-love.
The Genesis Picture.
God Giving Himself.
God's Fellow.
The Genesis Water-mark.
A Human Picture of God.
On a Wooing Errand.
Jesus' World-passion.

The Master Passion

The Earliest Calvary Picture.

There's a great passion burning in the heart of God. It is tenderly warm and tenaciously strong. Its fires never burn low, nor lose their fine glow. That passion is to win man back home again. The whole world of man is included in its warm, eager reach.

The old home hearth-fire of God is lonely since man went away. The family circle is broken. God will not rest until that old home circle is complete again, and every voice joining in the home songs.

It is an *overmastering* passion, the overmastering passion of God's heart. It has guided and controlled all His thoughts and plans for man from the first. The purpose of winning man, and the whole race, back again is the dominant gripping passion of God's heart to-day. Everything is made to bend to this one end.

When Eden's tragedy came so early, to darken the pages of this old Book, and, far worse, to darken the pages of human life, there is a great glimpse of this passion of God's heart in the guarding of those Eden gates. The presence of the angels with their sword of flame told plainly of a day when man would be coming back again to the old Eden home of God. The place must be carefully guarded for him.

This is a *love* passion, a passion of love. And love itself is the master passion both of the human heart and of God's heart. Nothing can grip and fill and sway the heart either of man or God like that.

We would all easily agree that the greatest picture of God's marvellous, overmastering passion of love is seen in the cross. All men as they have come to know that story have stood with heads bowed and bared before the love revealed there. They have not understood it. They have quarrelled about its meaning. But they have acknowledged its love and power as beyond that of any other story or picture.

However men may differ as to why Jesus died, and how His dying affects us, they all agree that the scene of the cross is the greatest revelation of love ever known or ever shown. All theories of the atonement seem to be lost sight of in one thought of grateful acknowledgment of a stupendous love, as men are drawn together by the magnetism of the hill-top of Calvary.

But there is a wondrously clear foreshadowing of that tremendous cross scene in the earliest page of this old Book. Nowhere is love, God's passion of love, made to stand out more distinctly and vividly than in the first chapter of Genesis. The after-scene of the cross uses intenser coloring;

the blacks are inkier in their blackness; the reds deeper and redder; the contrasts sharper to the startling-point; yet there is nothing in the cross chapters of the Gospels not included fully in this first leaf of revelation. But it has taken the light of the cross to open our eyes to see how much is plainly there. Let us look at it a bit.

The Love Passion.

What is this greatest of passions called love? There is no word harder to get a satisfactory definition of. Because, whatever you say about it, there comes quickly to your mind some one who loves you, or you think of the passion that burns in your own heart for some one. And, as you think of that, no words that anybody may use seem at all strong enough, or tender enough, to tell what love is, as you know it in your own inner heart.

Yet I think this much can be said—love is the tender, strong outgoing of your whole being to another. It is a passion burning like a fire within you, a soft-burning but intense fire within you, for some other one. Every mention of that name stirs the flame into new burning. Every passing or lingering thought of him or her is like fresh air making the flames leap up more eagerly. And each personal contact is a clearing out of all the ashes, and a turning on of all the draughts, to feed new oxygen for stronger, fresher burning.

There are many other things that seem like love. Kindliness and friendliness, and even intenser emotions, use love's name for themselves. But though these have likenesses to love, they are not love. They have caught something of its warm glow. A bit of the high coloring of its flames plays on them. But they are not the real thing, only distant kinsfolk. The severe tests of life quickly reveal their lack.

Love itself is really an aristocrat. It allows very, very few into its inner circle, often only one. The real thing of love is never selfish. Now we know very well that in the thick of life the fine gold of love gets mixed up with the baser metals. It is very often overlaid, and shot through with much that is mean and low. Rank selfishness, both the coarse kind and the refined, cultured sort, seeks a hiding-place under its cloak. But the stuff mixed in it is not love, but a defiling of it. That is a bit of the slander it suffers for a time, from the presence in life of sin.

Weeds with their poison, and snakes and spiders with their deadly venom, draw life from the sun. That is a bit of the bad transmuting the good, pure sun into its own sort. The sun itself never produces poison or any hurtful thing.

Love itself is never mean, nor bad, nor selfish. The man who truly loves the woman whom he would have for his own lifelong, closest companion is not selfish. He does not want her chiefly for his own sake, but for her sake, that so he may guard and care for her, and her life be fully grown in the sunlight of the love it must have. And, if you think that is idealizing it out of all practical

The Master Passion

reach, please remember that true love will steadily refuse the union that would not be best for the loved one.

What is the finest and highest love that we know? There are many different sorts and degrees of love revealed in man's relation with his fellow: conjugal, the love between husband and wife; paternal, the love of a father for his child; maternal, the mother's love for her child; filial, the love of children for father and mother; fraternal, or brotherly, meaning really the love of children of the same parents for each other, both brothers and sisters—the same word is used for love between friends where there is no tie of blood; and patriotic, or love for one's country. And under that last word may be loosely grouped the love that one may have for any special object, to which he may devote his life, outside of personal relationships, such as music or any profession or occupation.

This is putting them in their logical order. Though in our experience we know the father- and mother-love for ourselves first; and then in turn the others, so far as they come to us, until we complete the circle and reach the climax of father- and mother-love in ourselves going out to another.

Mother-love.

Now of these sorts and degrees which is the highest and finest? Well, your answer to that question will depend entirely on your own experience; as every answer and every thought we have of everything does. All children have mothers, or have had, but thousands of children don't know a mother's love.

I was speaking one time in New York City about the conception, of which the Bible is so full, that God is a mother. And the English evangelist Gypsy Smith, who lost his mother when very young, but who had an unusually devoted father, said with charming simplicity that he could not just see how God could be called a mother, but he knew He was a father. And then he went on to speak very winsomely of God as a father.

Many times love is not born in the heart at all, until there comes into the life some one clear outside of one's own kin. Many a woman never knows love until it is awakened in her heart by him who henceforth is to be a part of herself.

But the common answer, that most people everywhere give to that question, is that *a mother's love* is the greatest human love we know. And if you press them to tell why they think so, this stands out oftenest and strongest—that it is because she gives so much of herself. She gives her very life. If need be, she sacrifices everything in life, and then sacrifices life itself, going out into the darkness of death that her child may come into fulness and sweetness of life. This is the mother spirit, giving one's very self to bring life to another.

The mother gives her very life-blood that the new life may come. And, if need be, will gladly give her life *out* to the death that the new life may come into life. And yet more, she gives her life out daily and yearly, throughout its length, that so the full strength and fragrance of life may come in her child's life.

Yet, when all this has been said, I am strongly inclined to think that the mother's love, though the greatest that can be found in any one heart, is not the perfect, fully grown love. The human unit is not a man nor a woman, but a man *and* a woman. Perfect love requires more than one or two for its matured growth into full life. It cannot exist in its full strength and fragrant sweets except where three are joined together to draw out its full depth and meaning.

There must be two whose hearts are fully joined in love, each finding answering and ever-satisfying love in the other; and so each love growing to full ripeness in the warm sunshine of the other love. And then there needs to be a third one, who comes as a result of that mutual love, and who constantly draws out the love of the other two.

For love in itself is creative. It yearns to bring into being another upon whom it may freely lavish itself. That other one must be of its own sort, upon its own level. Nothing less ever satisfies. And so the love poured out draws out to itself an answering love fully as full as its own. And then, having yearned, it does more. It creates. It must create. It must bring forth life; and life like its own in all its powers and privileges. This is the very life of love in its full expression.

the finer, gentler, sweeter, maybe softer qualities, in the strong meaning of that word soft.

God Giving Himself.

Here in this Genesis story the creation of the whole sun-system to give life to the earth, and of the earth itself, was the outward beginning of this greatest passion of love in the heart of God. And if you would know more of that love in this early stage of it, just look a bit at the home itself. It has been pretty badly mussed, soiled and hurt by sin's foul touch. Yet even so it is a wonder of a world in its beauty and fruitfulness. What must it have been before the slime and tangle of sin got in! But that's a whole story by itself. We must not stop there just now.

When the home was ready God set Himself to bringing the new life He was planning. And He did it, even as father and mother of our human kind and of every other kind do:—He gave some of Himself. He breathed into man His own life-breath. He came Himself, and with the warmth and vitality of His life brought a new life. The new life was a bit of Himself.

That phrase, "breathed into his nostrils," brings to us the conception of the closest personal, physical contact; two together in most intimate contact, and life passing from one to the other. The picture of Elijah stretching his warm body upon that of the widow's son until the life-breath came again comes instinctively to mind. And its companion scene comes with it, of Elisha lying prone upon the child, mouth to mouth, eye to eye, hand to hand, until the breath again softly reentered that little, precious body.

And if all this seems too plain and homely a way to talk about the great God, let us remember it is the way of this blessed old Book. It is the only way we shall come to know the marvellous intimacy and tenderness of God's love, and of God's touch upon ourselves.

How shall we talk best about God so as to get clear, sensible ideas about Him? Why not follow the rule of the old Bible? Can we do better? It constantly speaks of Him in the language that we use of men. The scholars, with their fondness for big words, say the Bible is anthropomorphic. That simply means that it uses man's words, and man's ideas of things in telling about God. It makes use of the common words and ideas, that man understands fully, to tell about the God, whom he doesn't know. Could there be a more sensible way? Indeed, how else could man understand?

Some dear, godly people have sometimes been afraid of the use of simple, homely language in talking about God. To speak of Him in the common language of every-day life, the common talk of home and kitchen, and shop and street and trade, seems to them lacking in due reverence. Do they forget that this is the language of the common people? And of our good old Anglo-Saxon Bible? Has anybody ever yet used as blunt homely, talk as this old Book uses? And has any other book stuck into people's memories and hearts with such burr-like hold as it has?

That breathing by God into man's nostrils of the breath of life suggests the intensest concentration of strength and thought and heart. The whole heart of God went out to man in that breath that brought life.

God's Fellow.

The whole thought of God's heart was to have a man *like Himself*. Over and over again, with all the peculiar emphasis of repetition, it is said that the man was to be in the very image, or likeness, of God. God gave Himself that the man might be a bit of Himself. Here is the love-passion, the mother-passion, the father-mother-passion, in its highest mood, and at its own finest work.

The man was to be the very best, that so he might have fellowship of the most intimate sort with God. Of course, only those who are alike can have fellowship. Only in that particular thing which any two have in common can they have fellowship together. Let me use a common word in its old, fine, first meaning: man was made to be *God's fellow*, His most intimate associate and companion.

As you read this early story in Genesis of God's passion of love, you know, if you stop to think into it, that if ever the need for it came, He will climb any Calvary hill, however steep, and receive the jagging nails of any cross, however cutting, for the sake of His darling child—man.

This love-passion never faileth. There is no emergency that can arise that is too great for love's resources. Any danger, however great, every need, no matter how distressing, is already provided for by love. The emergency may sorely test and tax love to its last limit, but it can never outdo it, nor outstrip it in the race. No matter how great the danger, love is a bit greater. No matter how strong the enemy threatening, love is always yet stronger. However deep down into the very vitals of life the poison-sting may sink its fangs, love goes yet deeper, neutralizing the deadly influence with its own fresh life-blood.

Have you ever looked into a single drop of water and seen the sun? the whole of that brilliant ball of fire there in one tiny drop of water? Well, there's one word on this first leaf of the Book which contains the clear reflection, sharply outlined, of the whole creation story; ah! yes, more than that, of the whole Gospel story.

Come here and look; you can see in its clear surface the form of a man climbing a little, steep hill, and being hung, thorn-crowned, upon a cross of pain and shame. It is in chapter one, verse two, the word "brooding." The old version and the Revision, both English and American, have the word "moved." The Revisions add "brooding" in the margin. And that is the root meaning of the word underneath our English—"brooding," or, rendered more fully, "was brooding tremulous with love."

The Genesis Water-mark.

That English word "brooding," as well as the old word underneath, is a mother word. The brooding hen sits so faithfully, day after day, upon the eggs, bringing the new lives by the vital warmth of her own body. The mother-bird nestles softly down upon the nest in the crotch of the tree, patiently, expectantly brooding, by the strength of her own life giving life to the coming young. She who, in the holiest, greatest function entrusted to her, comes nearest to God in creative power and love—the mother of our human kind, broods for long months over her coming child, giving her very life, until the crisis of birth comes; and then broods still, for months and years longer, that the new life may come into fulness of life. That is the great word used here.

Now, will you please notice very keenly the connection in which it occurs. It was because the earth was "waste and void, and darkness upon the face of the deep," that the Spirit of God was brooding. It is only fair to say that our scholarly friends who think in Hebrew are divided as to the meaning here. Some think that these words, "waste and void," simply indicate a stage, or step, in the processes of creation.

But others of them are just as positive in saying that the words point plainly to a disaster of some sort that took place. In their view the whole story of creation is in the ten opening words of the chapter. Then follows a bad break of some sort;

The Master Passion

then the brooding of God in verse two; and the rest of the chapter is taken up in what is practically a reshaping up again of the whole affair. Some of this second group of Hebrew scholars have made this translation,—"the earth became a waste," or "a wreck," or "a ruin," or "without inhabitant."

If we may so read it now, it gives a world of additional meaning to this word "brooding." Here was love not merely giving life, but giving itself to overcome a disaster. The brooding was to mend a break. Love creates. It also redeems. It stoops down with great patience, and washes the dirt and filth thoroughly off, in the best cleansing liquid to be found, and brings the cleansed, redeemed man back again.

Love does indeed create. It gave man the power to choose freely, without any restriction, whatever he would choose to choose. Redeeming love does more. It woos him to choose the right, and only the right. It gets down by his side after his eyesight has become twisted, and his will badly kinked by wrong choosing, and patiently, persistently works to draw him up to the level of choosing right. Love makes us like God in the power of choice. But there's a greater task ahead. It makes us yet more like Him in the desire to choose only the right, and in the power to choose it, too. All this is in that marvellous world of a word—"brooding."

The whole story of the sacrifice of Calvary is included in this wondrous first leaf of revelation. If we had lost the Gospels, and didn't know their story, nor the history of man, we yet could know from this Genesis page that, if ever the need arose, God would lavishly give out His very life, at any cost of suffering and pain, that His man might be saved. John, three, sixteen is in the first chapter of Genesis. Calvary is in the creation. God gave His breath to man in creation, and His blood for man on Calvary. He gave His blood because He had given His breath. Each was His very life.

You know the way publishers have of putting an imprint in a book by means of what is called a water-mark. By the skilful use of water in manufacturing the paper, a name or trade imprint is made a part of the very paper of which the book is made.

Have you ever noticed God's water-mark on the paper of this first leaf of His Book? Hold your Bible up as we talk; separate this first leaf and hold it up to the light and try to see through it. The best light to use is that which came from Calvary. Can you see the water-mark plainly imprinted there? Look closely and carefully, for it is there. In clear-cut outline, every bit of it showing sharply out, is a cross. And if you look still more closely you will find this water-mark different from those in common use, in this— *there is a distinct blood-red tinge to it.*

A Human Picture of God.

Illustrations of God from our common life are never full, and must not be taken too critically,

The Master Passion

but they are sometimes wonderfully vivid and very helpful. Anything that makes God seem real and near helps.

A few years ago I heard a simple story of real life from the lips of a New England clergyman. It was told of a brother clergyman of the same denomination, and stationed in the same city with the man who told me.

This clergyman had a son, about fourteen years of age, who, of course, was going to school. One day the boy's teacher called at the house and asked for the father. When they met he said:

"Is your son sick?"

"No; why?"

"He was not at school to-day."

"You don't mean it!"

"Nor yesterday."

"Indeed!"

"Nor the day before."

"Well!"

"And I supposed he was sick."

"No, he's not sick."

"Well, I thought I should tell you."

And the father thanked him, and the teacher left. The father sat thinking about his son, and those three days. By and by he heard a click at the gate, and he knew the boy was coming in. So he went to the door to meet him at once. And the boy knew as he looked up that the father knew about those three days.

And the father said, "Come into the library, Phil."

And Phil went and the door was shut.

Then the father said very quietly, "Phil, your teacher was here a little while ago. He tells me you were not at school to-day, nor yesterday, nor the day before. And we thought you were. You let us think you were. And you don't know how bad I feel about this. I have always said I could trust my boy Phil. I always have trusted you. And here you have been a living lie for three whole days. I can't tell you how bad I feel about it."

Well, it was hard on the boy to be talked to in that gentle way. If his father had spoken to him roughly, or had taken him out to the wood-shed, in the rear of the dwelling, it wouldn't have been nearly so hard.

Then the father said, "We'll get down and pray." And the thing was getting harder for Phil all the time. He didn't want to pray just then. Most people don't about that time.

And they got down on their knees, side by side. And the father poured out his heart in prayer. And the boy listened. Somehow he saw himself in the looking-glass of his knee-joints as he hadn't before. It is queer about that mirror of the knee-joints, the things you see in it. Most people don't like to use it much. And they got up from their knees. The father's eyes were wet. And Phil's eyes were not dry.

Then the father said, "My boy, there's a law of life, that where there is sin there is suffering. You can't get those two things apart. Wherever there is suffering there has been sin, somewhere, by somebody. And wherever there is sin there will be suffering, for some one, somewhere; and likely most for those closest to you."

"Now," he said, "my boy, you have done wrong. So we'll do this. You go up-stairs to the attic. I'll make a little bed for you there in the corner. We'll bring your meals up to you at the usual times. And you stay up in the attic three days and three nights, as long as you've been a living lie." And the boy didn't say a word. They climbed the attic steps. The father kissed his boy, and left him alone.

Supper-time came, and the father and mother sat down to eat. But they couldn't eat for thinking of their son. The longer they chewed on the food the bigger and drier it got in their mouths. And swallowing was clear out of the question. And the mother said, "Why don't you eat?" And he said softly, "Why don't *you* eat?" And, with a catch in her throat, she said, "I can't, for thinking of Phil." And he said, "That's what's bothering me."

And they rose from the supper-table, and went into the sitting-room. He took up the evening paper, and she began sewing. His eyesight was not very good. He wore glasses, and to-night they seemed to blur up. He couldn't see the print distinctly. It must have been the glasses, of course. So he took them off, and wiped them with great care, and then found the paper was upside-down. And she tried to sew. But the thread broke, and she couldn't seem to get the thread into the needle again. How we all reveal ourselves in just such details!

By and by the clock struck ten, their usual hour of retiring. But they made no move to go. And the mother said quietly, "Aren't you going to bed?" And he said, "I'm not sleepy, I think I'll sit up a while longer; you go." "No, I guess I'll wait a while too." And the clock struck eleven; then the hands clicked around close to twelve. And they arose, and went to bed; but not to sleep. Each one pretended to be asleep. And each knew the other was not asleep.

After a bit she said—woman is always the keener—"Why don't you sleep?" And he said softly, "How did you know I wasn't sleeping? Why don't you sleep?" And she said, with that same queer catch in her voice, "I can't, for thinking of Phil." He said, "That's the bother with me." And the clock struck one; and then two; still no sleep. At last the father said, "Mother, I can't stand this. *I'm going up-stairs with Phil.*"

And he took his pillow, and went softly out of the room; climbed the attic steps softly, and pressed the latch softly so as not to wake the boy if he were asleep, and tiptoed across to the corner by the window. There the boy lay, wide-awake, with something glistening in his eyes, and what looked like stains on his cheeks. And the father got down between the sheets, and they got their arms around each other's necks, for they had always been the best of friends, and their tears got mixed up on each other's cheeks—you couldn't have told which were the father's and which the son's. Then they slept together until the morning light broke.

When sleep-time came the second night the father said, "Good-night, mother. I'm going up with Phil again." And the second night he shared his boy's punishment in the attic. And the third night when sleep-time came again, again he said, "Mother, good-night. I'm going up with the boy." And the third night he shared his son's punishment with him.

That boy, now a man grown, in the thews of his strength, my acquaintance told me, is telling the story of Jesus with tongue of flame and life of flame out in the heart of China.

Do you know, I think that is the best picture of God I have ever run across in any gallery of life? It is not a perfect picture. No human picture of God is perfect, except of course the Jesus human picture. The boy's punishment was arbitrarily chosen by the father, unlike God's dealings with our sin. But it is the tenderest and most real of any that has come to me.

God couldn't take away sin. It's here. Very plainly it is here. And He couldn't take away suffering, out of kindness to us. For suffering is sin's index-finger pointing out danger. It is sin's voice calling loudly, "Look out! there's something wrong." So He came down in the person of His Son, Jesus, and lay down alongside of man for three days and nights, in the place where sin drove man.

That's God! And that suggests graphically the great passion of His heart. Sin was not ignored. Its lines stood sharply out. The boy in the garret had two things burned into his memory, never to be erased: the wrong of his own sin, and the strength of his father's love.

Jesus is God coming down into our midst and giving His own very life, and then, more, giving it out in death, that He might make us hate sin, and might woo and win the whole world, away from sin, back to the intimacies of the old family circle again.

On a Wooing Errand.

Jesus was a mirror held up to the Father's face for man to look in. So we may know what the Father is like. When you look at Jesus and listen to Him you are looking into the Father's heart and listening to its warm throbbing. And no one can look there without being caught by the great passion burning there, and feeling its intense soft-burning glow, and carrying some of it for ever after in his own heart.

Jesus was on *a wooing errand* to the earth. The whole spirit of His dealings with men was that of a great lover, wooing them to the Father. He was insistently eager to let men know what His Father was like. He seemed jealous of His Father's reputation among men. It had been slandered badly. Men misunderstood the Father. He would leave no stone unturned to let men know how good and loving and winsome God

The Master Passion

is. For then they would eagerly run back home again to Him. This was His method of approach to the world He came to win.

Jesus is the greatest wooer the old world has ever known, and will be the greatest winner of what He is after, too. Run thoughtfully through these Gospels, and stand by Jesus' side in each one of these simple, tremendous incidents of His contact with the common people. Then listen anew to His teaching talks, so homely and so gripping. And the impression becomes irresistible that the one thought that gripped at every turn, never forgotten, was to woo man back to the Father's allegiance.

Jesus' World-passion.

Have you not marked *the world-wide swing* of Jesus' thought and plan? It is stupendous in its freshness and bold daring. The bigness of His idea of the thing to be done is immense. To use a favorite phrase of to-day, He had *a world-consciousness*. It is hard for us to realize what a startling thing His world-consciousness was. We are so familiar with the Gospels that we lose much of their force through mere rote of familiarity.

It takes a determined effort, and the fresh touch of the Holy Spirit, too, to have them come with all the freshness of a new book. And then we have gotten sort of used in our day, and in our part of the world especially, to talking about world-wide enterprises.

We don't realize what a stupendous thing a world-consciousness was in Jesus' day. He certainly did not get it from His own generation; not from the Jews. It stands out in keen contrast to their ideas. They lived within very narrow alleyways. They supposed they were the favorites of God; and everybody else—*dogs*, and *damned* dogs, too; not in the profane usage, but actually.

But Jesus thought of a *world*, and yearned for a world. The words "world" and "earth" are constantly on His lips. He said He came "into the world;" not to Palestine; that was only the door He used for entrance. It was from Him that John learned, what he wrote down, that He was to "lighten *every man* that cometh into *the world*."

To the Jewish senator of the inner national circle He said plainly in that great sentence that contains the gist of the whole Bible—John, three sixteen—that it was *a world* he was after. *A saved world* was the one purpose of His errand to the earth. He had come to "*save the world*,"[1] and would stop at nothing short of giving His very self "for the life of *the world*."

He tells His own inner circle that "the field" is a *world*. And that it is to be won by the means He Himself was using; namely, men, human beings, "sons of the kingdom"[2] were to be sown as seed all over its vast extent.

[1] John 3:17.
[2] Matthew 13:38.

The Master Passion

You remember, that last week, the request of the Greeks for an interview?[1] The outside non-Jewish world came to Him in the visit and earnest request of those Greeks. And His whole being became greatly agitated. It was as when one, at last, after years of labor without any seeming success, gets a first faint glimpse of the results he longs so earnestly for. Here was a touch, a glimpse of the very thing on which His heart was so set. The great outside world was coming to Him.

The realization of its tremendous meaning, the sure promise it held of the day when *all the world would be coming* seems to set Him all a-tremble with intensest emotion. The delight of the possible realizing of His life-dream, His earth errand, and yet the terrific conviction that only by travelling the red road of the cross could that world be won, made a fierce conflict within. It was the world-vision that agitated Him.

And it was that same world-vision that held Him steady. He would not scatter. By concentrating all in one act He would generate and set off a dynamic power on Calvary that would shake and then shape a world. The knowledge that all men would be irresistibly drawn by the loadstone of the cross steadied His steps.

A few days later, as He sat resting a bit, on the side of the Hill of Olivet, the disciples earnestly ask for some idea of His plan. And He explains that the Gospel was to be "preached to the

[1] John 12:20-33.

whole inhabited earth."[1] That conception was never out of His mind. How could it be!

But the great purpose and passion of His life stands out most sharply in the words of that last imperial command. He shows the whole of His heart in that stirring "Go ye into *all the world* and make disciples of *all the nations*"; "preach the gospel to *the whole creation.*" The passion of Jesus' heart was to win the world. And that passion has grown intenser in waiting. To-day more than ever the one passion of yonder enthroned Man is to win His world. Everything else bends to that with Him. Nothing less will satisfy His heart.

Now, the God-touched man is always swayed by the same purpose and passion as sway God. The passion of every God-touched man, fresh from direct contact with Him, is to win the whole world up to God. Everything will be held under the strong thumb of this, and made to fit and bend and blend into it.

[1] Matthew 24:14.

THE MASTER'S PLAN

Will the World Be Won?
Some Bad Drifts.
Great Incidental Blessings.
The World Really Lost.
God's Method of Saving.
The Programme of World-winning.
Early Moorings.
Service Unites.
The World-winning Climb.

The Plan

Will the World Be Won?

The great passion of God's heart is a love-passion. Love never fails. It waits and, if need be, waits long; but it never fails to get what it is waiting for. Love sacrifices; though it never uses that word. It doesn't know it *is* sacrificing, it is so absorbed in its gripping purpose. There may be keen-cutting pain, but it is clean forgotten in the passion that burns within. God means to win His world of men back home to Himself.

But some earnest friend is thinking of an objection to all this talk about a world being won. You are taken all anew with the great picture of God's passion of love in the opening page of this old Book. But all the time we have been talking together you have been having a crosscutting train of thought underneath. It has been saying, "Isn't this going a bit too far? will the whole world be won?"

Let us talk over that a bit. We have been used all our lives to hearing about *soul-winning*. We have been urged, more or less, to do it. A favorite motto in some Christian workers' convention has been, "Win one." But this idea of winning the world has not been preached. At first it doesn't seem exactly orthodox.

The old-time preaching, of which not so much is heard now, except in restricted quarters, is that the whole world is lost; and that we are to save people out of it. We used to be told that the world is bad, and only bad; bad beyond redemption, and doomed. In his earlier years Mr. Moody used to say often with his great earnestness that this was a doomed world, and that the great business of life was to save men out of it.

But of late years there has been a distinct swing away from this sort of preaching and talking. Everything we humans do seems to go by the clock movement, the pendulum swing: first one side, then the other. Now we hear a very different sort of preaching. This is really a good world. There is some wickedness in it, to be sure. Indeed, there is quite a great deal of it. But in the main it is not a bad world, we're told.

The old-time preaching was chiefly concerned with getting ready for heaven. Now it is concerned, for most part, with living pure, true lives right here on the earth. And that change is surely a good one. But it is also the common thing to be told that the world is not nearly so bad as we have been led to believe.

Some Bad Drifts.

It is striking that with that has come a change of talk about sin, the thing that was supposed to be responsible for making the world so bad. Sin

The Plan 39

is not such a damnable thing now, apparently. It is largely constitutional weakness, or prenatal predilection, or the idiosyncrasy of individuality. (Big words are in favor here. They always make such talk seem wise and plausible.) Heaven has slipped largely out of view; and—hell, too, even more. Churchmen in the flush of phenomenal material prosperity, with full stomachs and luxurious homes and pews, are well content with things as they are in this present world, and don't propose to move.

And with that it is easy to believe what we are freely told, that there is really no need of giving our Christian religion to the heathen world. Those peoples have religions of their own that are remarkably good. At least they are satisfactory to them. Why disturb them? They are doing very well. This talk about their being lost, and needing a Savior, is reckoned out of date. The old common statements about so many thousands dying daily, and going out into a lost eternity, are not liked. They are called lurid. And, indeed, they are not used nearly so much now as once.

This swing away has had a great influence upon the mass of church-members, and upon their whole thought of the foreign-mission enterprise. There is a vaguely expressed, but distinctly felt idea both in the Church and outside of it, for the two seem to overlap as never before—that the sending of missionaries is really not to save peoples from being lost. That sort of talk is almost vulgar now.

Mission work is really a sort of good-natured

neighborliness. It is benevolent humanitarianism in which we may all help, more or less (usually less), regardless of our beliefs or lack of beliefs, our church-membership or attendance. We should show these heathen our improved methods of living. We have worked out better plans of housekeeping and schooling, of teaching and doctoring, and farming and all the rest of it. And now we want to help these poor deficient peoples across the seas.

We think we are a superior people in ourselves, as well as in our type of civilization, decidedly so. And having taken good care of ourselves, and laid up a good snug sum, we can easily afford to help these backward far-away neighbors a bit. It is really the thing to do.

Such seems to be the general drift of much of the present-day talk about foreign missions. The Church, and its members individually, have grown so rich that we have forgotten that we were ever poor. The table is so loaded with dainties that we are quite willing to be generous with the crumbs, even cake crumbs.

Great Incidental Blessings.

Now, without doubt the sending of the missionaries has vastly improved conditions of human life in the foreign-mission lands. The missionaries have been the forerunners of great improvements. They have been the pioneers blazing out the paths along which both trade and diplomacy have gone with the newer and better

The Plan

civilization of the West. Civilization has developed marvellously in the western half of the world. And the missionaries have been its advance agents into the stagnant East, and the savage wilds of the southern hemisphere.

Full, accurate knowledge of nature's resources and laws, and adaptation of that knowledge to practical uses, have been among the most marked conditions of the western world during the past century. And, as a result, education, medical and hygienic and sanitary science, development of the earth's soil, and resources above and below the soil, have gone forward by immense strides. So far as is known, our progress in such matters exceeds all previous achievements in the history of the race.

And some of all this has been seeping into the heathen world. It hasn't gotten in far yet; only into the top soil, and about the edges, so far. The progress in this regard has seemed both rapid and slow. When the great mass of these peoples have not yet gotten even a whiff of the purer, better civilization air of the western nations the progress seems slow. But when we remember the incalculably tremendous inertia, and the strangely stagnant spirit of heathen lands, it seems rapid.

The effort to get the heathen world simply to clean up; to open the windows and let in some fresh air, and use plain soap and water to scrub off the actual dirt makes one think of the typical small boy's dislike of being washed up. It has been a hard job. Yet a great beginning has been made. The boy seems to be beginning to find out that his face *is* dirty, and *feels* dirty. And that is an enormous gain.

The World Really Lost.

Yet while this is good, and only good, it isn't the thing we are driving at in missions. While it would fully warrant all the expenditures of money, and vastly more than has yet been given, it should be said in clearest, most ringing tones that all this is *merely incidental.* It is blessed. It is sure to come. It is remarkable that it always has come where the Gospel of Jesus is preached.

Yet this is not the thing aimed at in missions. The one driving purpose is to carry to men *a Saviour from sin.* And to take Him so earnestly and winsomely that men yonder shall be wooed and won to the real God, whom they have lost knowledge of.

It cannot be said too plainly that the world *is* lost. It has strayed so far away from the Father's house that it has lost all its bearings, and can't find its way back without help. The old preaching that this is a lost world, is true.

But we need to remember the different uses of that word "world." In the old-time conception it was used in a loose way as meaning the spirit that actuates men in the world. The scheme of selfishness and wickedness and sinfulness which has overcast all life is commonly spoken of in the Bible as the world spirit. In that sense the

The Plan

world is bad, and only bad. Men are to be saved out of it, as Moody said.

But, in the other commoner use of it, that word "world" simply means the whole race of men. And we must remind ourselves vigorously of the plain truth that this is a lost world. That is to say, men have gotten away from God. They completely misunderstand Him. Then they do more, and worse, they misrepresent and slander Him. The result is complete lack of trust in Him. They have lost their moorings, and have drifted out to deep sea with no compass on board. Thick fogs have risen and shut out sun and stars and every guiding thing. They are hopelessly and helplessly lost, and need some one to bring the compass so as to get back to shore, back home to God.

But this world of men is to be won. Jesus said He came to save a world. And He will not fail nor rest content until He has done it, and this has become a saved world. He said that He gave His life for the life of the world. And the world will yet know the fulness of that life of His throbbing in its own heart.

This does not mean that all men will be saved. There seems to be clear evidence in the Book that some will insist on preferring their own way to God's. And I am sure I do not know anything except what the Book teaches. It is the only reliable source of information I have been able to find so far. It must be the standard, because it is the standard.

There will be a group of stubborn irreconcilables holding out against all of God's tender pleading. John's Patmos vision of glory, with its marvellous beauty and sweep, has yet a lake of fire and a group of men insisting upon going their own way. If a man choose that way, he may. He is still in the likeness of God in choosing to leave out God. He remains a sovereign in his own will even in the hell of his own choosing.

God's Method of Saving.

The method of saving is by *winning*. The Father would not be content with anything else. Such a thing as might be represented by throwing a blanket over the head of a horse in a burning stable, and so getting it out by coaxing, and forcing, and hiding the danger, is not to be thought of here. Sin is never smoothed over by God, nor its results, their badness and their certainty.

He would have us see the sin as ugly and damning as it actually is, and see Him as pure and holy and winsome as He is; and then to reject the sin and choose Himself. The method of much modern charity, the long-range charity that helps by organization, without the personal relation and warm touch, is unknown to God. He touches every man directly with His own warm heart, and appeals to Him at closest quarters.

Man's highest power is his power of choosing. It is in that He is most like God. God's plan is to clear away the clouds, sweep down the cobwebs that bother our eyes so, and let us get such a look

The Plan

at Himself that we will be caught with the sight of His great face, and choose to come, and to come a-running back to Himself. The world will be saved by its own choosing to be. It will be saved by being won. Men will choose to leave sin and accept God's Saviour Jesus Christ.

It is a great method. It is the only method God could use. The creative love-passion of His heart was that we should choose Himself in preference to all else, and choose life with Him up on His level as the only life.

And the method of winning is by getting each man's consent. The old cry of soul-winning is the true cry. It tells the method of work for us to follow. Each man is to be won by his own free glad consent. There is to be no wholesaling except by retailing. In business the wholesale comes after the retail. It is the child and servant of the retail.

Here the method is to be one by one; and the results, a great multitude beyond the power of any arithmetic to count. Soul-winning is the method, and world-winning is the object and the final result.

The Programme of World-winning.

There is *a programme of world-winning* repeatedly outlined in this old Book of God. That programme has not always been clearly understood. Indeed, it may be said that for the most part it has been misunderstood, and still is by many. And, as a result, many churchmen have lost their bearings, and strayed far from the Master's plan for their own lives and service. It helps greatly to get the programme clear in mind, so we can steer a straight course, and not get confused nor lost.

The first item of that programme is world-wide evangelization. That is the great service and privilege committed to the Church, and to every Christian, for this present time. Every other service is second to this. This does not mean world-wide conversion. That comes later. It does mean a full, winsome telling of the story of Jesus' Gospel, to all nations and to all men.

It means the doing of it by all sorts of helpful, sensible means; the hospital and medical dispensary, the school and college, the printed page, and the practical helping of men in every way that they can be helped. Above all, it means the warm, sympathetic, brotherly touch. Not simply by preaching; that surely, but in addition to that the practical preaching of the Gospel by all of these means.

When that has been accomplished the Kingdom will come. The King will come, and with Him the Kingdom. There will be radical changes in all the moral conditions of the earth. It will be a time of greatly increased evangelization, and of conversions of people in immense numbers. It will seem as if all were giving glad allegiance to Jesus the King. The world will then seem to be indeed a won world.

But there will be many who have simply been swung into line outwardly by the general movement among the mass of peoples, just as it always is. And our King wants whole-hearted love and service.

And so, at the end of the kingdom period, there will come another crisis. It is spoken of by John in his Revelation vision[1] as a loosing of Satan, and a renewal of his activity among men. That used to puzzle me a good bit. I wondered why, when that foul fiend had once been securely fastened up, he should be loosed again. But I'm satisfied that the reason is that at the end of the Kingdom time there is to be full opportunity for those who are not at heart loyal to Jesus, and who simply bow to Him because the crowd is doing so, to be perfectly free to do and go as they choose.

Jesus wants a *heart* allegiance, and only that. The great thing is that every man shall freely choose as he really prefers. This it is that both makes and reveals character. And so there will be a final crisis. All who at heart prefer to do so may swing away from Jesus.

That crisis ends with the final and overwhelming defeat of Satan and all the forces of evil. He goes to his own place, the place he has chosen and made for himself; and all who prefer to leave God out will go by the moral gravitation of their own choice to that place with him.

Then follows the full vision of a won world, which John pictures in such glowing colors in these last two chapters of Revelation, as a city come down from God out of heaven.

[1] Revelation 20:7-8.

Early Moorings.

There are two leading passages that speak of this programme. You remember that during the last week of His life Jesus told His disciples of the fall of Jerusalem. They came earnestly asking for fuller information regarding the future events. They asked when the present period of time would come to an end. And in answering He said—and the answer became a pivotal passage around which much else swings—that the Gospel of the Kingdom would be preached in the whole inhabited earth for a testimony unto all nations. And then the end of the present age or period of time would come.[1]

The first council of the Christian Church was held as a result of the remarkable success attending the beginning of world-wide evangelization. It was held in Jerusalem to consider the serious question of what to do with the great multitude of foreign or Gentile converts.

The Church had been practically a Jewish church. But Paul had commenced his remarkable series of world-wide preaching-tours. Great numbers of the outside peoples had accepted Christ, and been organized into Christian churches. Some of the Jewish Church in Jerusalem thought that all of these should become Jewish in their observance of the old Mosaic requirements. Both Paul and Peter, the two great church leaders, object to this.

[1] Matthew 24:14.

The Plan

It is at the close of the conference that James, who was presiding, outlines in his decision the programme of world-winning of which we are talking together.[1] He quotes from the prophecy of Joel. He says there are to be three steps or stages in working out God's plan.

First of all is the preaching of the Gospel of Jesus to all the nations, in which work Paul had been so earnestly engaged, and the remarkable success of which it was that had given rise to the whole discussion. When this has been completed the kingdom is to be established with the nation of Israel in the central place, the tabernacle of David set up, as he quotes it. The purpose of this is that all the rest of the peoples on the earth, all the nations, "may *seek* after the Lord."

The purpose of the Kingdom is the same, in the main, as is now the purpose of the Church. It is to push forward on broader lines, and more vigorously than ever, the work of bringing all men back to the Father's house.

There are many other passages that might be referred to, but these will answer our purpose just now. There is to be a won world, and the old Book outlines plainly just how and when it will be won.

Service Unites.

Now, I know that all ministers and Christian teachers are not agreed about this. There has been a controversy in the Church, both long and

[1] Acts 15:13-18.

sometimes bitter, unfortunately, about the Lord's return and the setting up of the Kingdom. And I have no desire to take any part in that, but instead, a strong desire to keep out of it. There is too much pressing emergency among men for helpful service to spend any time or strength in controversy.

In a word it may be put this way. There are those who believe that Jesus' coming is a thing to be expected as likely to occur at any time, or within our lifetime, within any generation. His coming is to be the beginning of the Kingdom period, when all peoples will be loyal to Him.

The others believe that the preaching of the Gospel will bring the whole world into allegiance, and that will be the Kingdom, and then Jesus will return. Both agree fully that the thing to be desired, and that will come, is the world-wide acknowledgment of Jesus as Saviour and King.

It may be added, however, that of later years there is a third great group in the Church, which is really the largest of the three. These people practically ignore the teaching about an actual return of Jesus to the earth. They believe that He has already come, and is continually coming in the higher ideals, the better standards, and nobler spirit that pervade society.

If it be true that the present preaching of the Gospel is to result in winning the whole world at once, without waiting for this programme of which I have spoken, then there is in that a very strong

The Plan

argument for world-wide evangelization. For only so can the desired result be secured. And so we can heartily join hands together in service regardless of what we believe on this question. I make a rule not to ask a man on which side of the question he stands, but to work with him hand in hand so far as I can in spreading the glad good news of Jesus everywhere.

The difference of view regarding the Lord's return need not affect the practical working together of all earnest men. We are perfectly agreed that the great thing is to have the story of Jesus' dying and rising again told out earnestly and lovingly to all men. And we can go at that with greatest heartiness, side by side.

The great concern now is to make Jesus fully known. That is the plan for the present time. It is a simple plan. Men who have been won are to be the winners. Nobody else can be. The warm enthusiasm of grateful love must burn in the heart and drive all the life. There must be simple, but thorough organization.

The campaign should be mapped out as thoroughly as a Presidential campaign is organized here in our country. The purpose of a Presidential campaign is really stupendous in its object and sweep. It is to influence quickly, up to the point of decisive action, the individual opinion of millions of men, spread over millions of square miles, and that, too, in the face of a vigorous opposing campaign to influence them the other way. The whole vast district of country is mapped out and organized on broad lines and into the smallest details.

Strong brainy men give themselves wholly to the task, and spend hundreds of thousands of dollars within a few months. And then, four years later, they proceed as enthusiastically as before to go over the whole ground again. We need as thorough organizing, as aggressive enthusiasm, and as intelligent planning for this great task which our Master has put into our hands.

And we have a driving motive power greater than any campaign-manager ever had or has—*a Jesus* who sets fire to one's whole being, with a passion of love that burns up every other flame. We need a Church as thoroughly organized, and every man in it with a burning heart for this great service.

The World-winning Climb.

An old school-master, talking to his class one morning, many years ago, told a story of an early experience he had had in Europe. He was one of a party travelling in Switzerland. They had gotten as far as Chamounix, and were planning to climb Mont Blanc. That peak, you know, is the highest of the Alps, and is called the monarch of European mountains. While it is now ascended every day in season, the climb is a very difficult task.

It requires strength and courage and much special preparation; and is still attended with

The Plan 53

such danger that the authorities of Chamounix have laid down rigid regulations for those who attempt it. One's outfit must be reduced to the very lowest limit. And, of course, nothing else can be done while climbing. It absorbs all one's strength and thought.

There were two parties in the little square of the town, making their preparations with the guides. One young Englishman disregarded all the directions of the guides. He loaded himself with things which he positively declared were absolutely essential to his plans.

He had a small case of wine and some delicacies for his appetite. He had a camera with which he proposed to take views of himself and his party at different stages of the climb. He had a batch of note-books in which he intended recording his impressions as he proceeded, which were afterward to be printed for the information, and, he hoped, admiration of the world. A picturesque cap and a gayly colored blanket were part of his outfit.

The old toughened guides, experienced by many a severe tug and storm in the difficulties ahead, protested earnestly. But it made no impression on the ambitious youth. At last they whispered together, and allowed him to have his own way. And the party started.

Six hours later the second party followed. At the little inn where they spent the first night they found the wine and food delicacies. The guides laughed. "The Englishman has found that he cannot humor his stomach if he would climb Mont Blanc," one of them said grimly. A little farther up they found the note-book and camera; still higher up, the gay robe and fancy cap had been abandoned. And at last they found the young fellow at the summit in leather jacket, exhausted and panting for breath.

He had encountered heavy storms, and reached the top of the famous mountain only at the risk of his life. But he reached it. He had the real stuff in him, after all. Yet everything not absolutely essential had to be sacrificed. And his ideas of the meaning of that word "essential" underwent radical changes as he labored up the steep.

Then the old teacher telling the story suddenly leaned over his desk and, looking earnestly at the class, said, "When I was young I planned out my life just as he planned out his climb. Food and clothing, and full records of my experiences for the world's information, figured in big. But at forty I cared only for such clothes as kept me warm, and at fifty only for such food as kept me strong. And so steep was the climb up to the top I had set my heart upon that at sixty I cared little for the opinions of people, if only I might reach the top. And when I do reach it I shall not care whether the world has a record of it or not. That record is in safety above."

We laugh at the ambitious young Englishman. But will you kindly let me say, plainly, without meaning to be critical in an unkind sense, that

The Plan

most of us do just as he did. And will you listen softly, while I say this—many of us, when we find we can't reach the top with our loads, let the top go, and pitch our tents in the plain, and settle down with our small plans and accessories. The plain seems to be quite full of tents.

The plan of the Swiss guides is *the plan* for the life-climb. It is *the* plan, and the only one for us to follow in the world-winning climb. That was Jesus' plan. He left behind and threw away everything that hindered, and at the last threw away life itself, that so the world might find life. We must follow Him.

THE URGENT NEED

THREE GREAT GROUPS.
THE NEEDLE OF THE COMPASS OF NEED.
A QUICK RUN ROUND THE WORLD.
WEST BY WAY OF THE EAST.
CHRISTIAN LANDS.
THE GREATEST NEED.
GROPING IN THE DARK.
LIVING MESSAGES OF JESUS.
THE GREAT UNKNOWN LACK.

The Need

Three Great Groups.

THE human heart is tender. It answers quickly to the cry of need. It is oftentimes hard to find. In Christian lands it is covered up with selfishness. And in heathen lands the selfishness seems so thickly crusted that it is hard to awaken even common humanitarian feeling.

But that heart once dug out, and touched, never fails to respond to the cry of need. We know how the cry of physical distress, of some great disaster, or of hunger will be listened to, and how quickly all men respond to that. When the terrible earthquake laid San Francisco in burning ruins the whole nation stopped, and gave a great heart-throb; and then commenced at once sending relief. Corporations that are rated soulless and men that are spoken of as money-mad, knocking each other pitilessly aside in their greed for gold and power, all alike sent quick and generous help of every substantial sort.

Beside expressing their sympathy in kindest and keenest word, they gave millions of dollars. Yet this might seem to be a family affair, as indeed it was. But the great famines in India and in other foreign lands farthest removed from us, have awakened a like response in our hearts. Great sums have been given in money and supplies to feed the hunger of far-away peoples, and help them sow their fields and get a fresh start.

There is a need far deeper and greater than that of physical suffering. And there is a heart far more tender than the best human heart. That need is to know God, whom to know is to enter into fulness of life, both physical and mental; and into that life of the spirit that is higher and sweeter than either of these lower down. And that tender heart is the human heart touched by the warm heart of God.

Many of us Christian people who are gathered here to-night have had unusual blessing in having our hearts touched into real life by the touch of God. And there's much more of the same sort waiting our fuller touch with Him. And now we want to see to-night something of the needs of God's great world-family, which is our own family because it is God's. Then we shall respond to it as freely and quickly and intelligently, as He Himself did and does.

I am going to ask you to come with me for a brief journey around the world. We want to get something of a clear, even though rapid view, of the whole of this world of ours. For the whole world is a mission field. Missionaries are sent everywhere, including our own home-land, and including all of our cities.

Our cities are as really mission fields as are the heathen lands. There is a difference, but it is only one of degree. The Christian standards present in our American life, and absent from these foreign-mission lands, make an enormous difference. But, apart from that great fact, the need of mission service is as really in New York as it is in Shanghai.

If we are to pray for the whole world, and to help in other ways to win it, we ought to try to get something of a clear idea of it, to help us in our thinking and praying and planning.

It will help toward that if we remember at the outset that the world from the religious point of view, divides up easily into three great groups. First there are the great non-Christian, or heathen, lands and nations. This includes those called Mohammedan; for, while that religion is based upon a partial Christian truth, it is so utterly corrupt in teaching and morally foul in practice that it is distinctly classed with the heathen religions.

Then there are the lands and nations under the control of those two great mediæval historic forms of Christianity, the Roman and Greek Churches, in which the vital principles of the Christian life seem to have been almost wholly lost in a network of forms and organization. The essential truths are there. But they are hidden away and covered up. There are untold numbers of true Christians there, but they live in a strangely clouded twilight

The Needle of the Compass of Need.

Let us look a little at these peoples. Where shall we start in? The old rule of the Master's command, and of the early Church's practice, was to begin "at Jerusalem," and keep moving until the outmost limit of the world was reached. I suppose that practically, in service, beginning at Jerusalem means beginning just where you are, and then reaching out to those nearest, and then less near, until you have touched the farthest.

But the old Jerusalem rule will make a good geographical rule for us English-speaking people, with an ocean between us, in getting a fresh look at this old world that the Master asks us to carry in our hearts and on our hands. So we'll begin there.

The needle of a magnetic compass always points north. The needle of the compass of progress has always pointed west; at least always since the Medo-Persian was the world-power. But it is striking that the compass of the world's *need* always points its needle toward the east. And so, starting at Jerusalem, we may well turn our faces east as we take our swing around the world to learn its need.

It may be a relief to you to know at once that there will not be any statistics in this series of talks. We want instead just now to get broad and general, but distinct, impressions. Statistics are burdensome to most people. They are a good deal of a bugbear to the common crowd of us every-day folks. They are absolutely essential. They are of immense, that is, immeasurable, value. You need to have them at hand where you can easily turn for exact information, as you need it, to refresh your memory. And an increasing amount of it will stick in your memory and guide your thinking and praying.

There are easily available, in these days of such remarkable missionary activity, an abundance of fresh statistics, in attractive form. We are greatly indebted to the Student Volunteer Movement and the Young People's Missionary Movement and the Church Societies for the great service they have done in this matter of full fresh information.

But the thing of first importance is to get an intelligent thought of the *whole world*. And then to add steadily to our stock of particular information, as study and prayer and service call for it. It is possible to get a simple grasp of the whole world. And it helps immensely to do it.

It helps at once to this end to remember that two-thirds of all the peoples of the earth are in the distinctly heathen, or non-Christian, lands. This in itself is a tremendous fact, telling at once of the world's need. At the beginning of the twentieth hundred-years since Jesus gave His command to preach His Gospel to all men, two-thirds of them are still in ignorance of Him and under the same moral sway as when He went away.

I might add that there are a billion people in these two-thirds. But that figure is so big as only to stagger the mind in an attempt to take it in. The important thing is to see that it doesn't by its sheer bigness, stagger our faith or our courage or our praying habit. We want to be like the old Hebrew who "staggered not" at God's promise to do for him a naturally impossible thing. Yet it is well to repeat that word "billion," for it brings up sharply and gigantically the staggering need of the world for Christ.

One-third is in lands commonly called Christian. Though we must use that word "Christian" in the broadest and most charitable sense in making that statement.

A Quick Run Round the World.

Beginning at Jerusalem, then, means for us just now beginning with the Turkish Empire. And with that, in this rapid run through, we may for convenience group Arabia and Persia and Afghanistan. This is the section where Mohammedanism, that corrupt mixture of heathenism with a small tincture of Christian truth, has its home, and whence it has gone out on its work throughout the world.

Great populations here have practically no knowledge at all of the Gospel, for missionary work is extremely scant. The land of the Saviour, with its eastern neighbors, has no Saviour, so far as knowing about Him is concerned, though it needs His saving very sorely.

The Need

Next to it, on the east, lies the great land of India, with the smaller countries that naturally group with it. And here are gathered fully *a fifth* of the people of the earth. These are really in large part our blood-brothers. Their fathers away back were brothers to our fathers. And so missionary work here ought to be reckoned largely as a family affair. British rule has had an immense humanizing influence here. Missionary activity has been carried on aggressively for years, and great and blessed progress has been made.

Yet it is merely a preparation for the work now so sorely needed. These years of faithful seed-sowing have made the soil dead ripe for a harvest in our day. A strange religiousness utterly lacking both in religion and in morality, abominably repugnant in its gross immorality, honeycombs the life of these people. The cry of need here is deep and pathetic.

Pushing on still to the east, the great land of China with its dependencies, looms up in all its huge giant size. Roughly speaking, almost *a third* of the world's people are grouped here. There are practically almost as many in what is reckoned Chinese territory as in all Christian lands. Here is found the oldest and best civilization of the non-Christian sort. The old common religion of Confucius is practically not a religion at all, but a code of maxims and rules, and utterly lacking in moral uplift or power.

The peculiarly impressive thing about China,

as indeed about nearly all of the heathen world, is *the spirit of stagnation.* There is a deadness, or sort of stupor, over everything. It is as if a blight had spread over the land, checking all progress. Habits, customs, and institutions remain apparently as they were a thousand years ago. This stands out in sharp contrast with the spirit of growth that marks Christian lands.

It seems strange to us because the spirit of growth is the atmosphere of our western world, breathed in from infancy. The one word that seems peculiarly to describe China is that word "stagnant." The people themselves are remarkable both for their mental power and their habits of industry. The Chinese may well be called the Anglo-Saxons of the Orient, in latent power and mental character.

In our modesty we think the Anglo-Saxon, the English-speaking, the greatest of living peoples. Certainly the leadership of the world is in Anglo-Saxon hands, and has been for centuries. And the marvellous, unprecedented progress of the world has been under that leadership.

Well, when these Chinese wake up we are very likely to find the race getting a new leadership, and the history of the world a new chapter added. What sort of leadership it will be morally, and what sort of a chapter, will depend on how much statesmanship there is in our praying and giving and missionary service. But the need is enormously intensified by the unawakened power of these Chinese.

West by Way of the East.

Still moving east, we come to the newly awakened and very attractive island-nation of Japan, which, because of its geographical and territorial situation, has been called the Great Britain of the Orient. Japan stands at present as the exception to the common stagnation of the heathen world. It has made a record nothing less than phenomenal as a student of Western life. It has absorbed, and imitated, and adapted to its own use, the Western knowledge and spirit with a wonderful power and intelligence.

Japan is both bright and ambitious to an almost abnormal degree, and as tricky in its dealings, and morally unclean in its life, as it is bright and ambitious. They have been called the Frenchmen of the Orient, and that characterization fits remarkably in many respects. Great progress has been made in giving the Gospel to Japan, but the present moral need is immensely intensified by the very aggressiveness of the Japanese spirit.

With Japan, the island-kingdom, it is easy to group the whole island-world lying to the east and south, though these are utterly different peoples. This includes the great number of islands scattered throughout the Pacific Ocean. The conditions are largely those of savagery except where affected by Christian civilization through the missionary enterprise. The Gospel has done some wonderful feats of transformation here. And there is plenty of room for more. Australia, the "island continent,"

68   Quiet Talks With World Winners

is a British colony, and of course now reckoned among Christian lands; as is also the large island of New Zealand, also a British colony, which has been a leader in some of the most advanced steps of modern civilization.

Crossing the Pacific to the east brings up the South American Continent; and Central America, the connecting stretch of land with our own continent; and Mexico, which is commonly grouped with foreign-mission lands. South America has been spoken of both as the "neglected continent" and as the "continent of opportunity." The common characteristic religiously of all this vast section from Mexico to the "Land of Fire," at the southernmost toe of South America, is that it is under the sway of the Roman Catholic Church. Some parts of it have been spoken of as "baptized heathenism." A vast network of church forms and organization, practically lifeless, holds these peoples in an iron grasp. The need of the Gospel of Jesus is fully as great as in civilized China or savage Africa.

One more long easterly stride, across the Atlantic, brings black Africa, and completes this rapid run around the globe, so far as distinctly heathen lands are concerned. Africa is peculiarly the savage continent, though it has the oldest civilization in its northeast corner, and the newest British civilization rapidly developing on its southern edge. It is the "dark continent," both in the color of its inhabitants and in its sad destitution and degradation. About *a tenth* of the world's population is here; with as many missionaries as in civilized India, but unable to reach the people as effectually as there because of the lack of national organization and the absence of great highways of travel.

Africa is essentially a great mass of separate tribes, larger and smaller, most of them in deepest savagery, with sorest need not only of salvation, but of civilization. The sore need of its very savagery has seemed to make it a magnet to missionary enterprise. And yet all that has been done, and is being done, seems almost swallowed up in the depth of its degradation and savagery.

I have taken you with me in this very rapid run that we might try to get a simple practical grasp of the heathen world. And if you and I might often take just such a run, with map or globe and Bible at hand, and our knees bent, it would greatly help us in getting close to the world our Lord died for; and which He means to win; and to win through you and me; and which He *will* win.

Christian Lands.

But I must talk with you a bit about our Christian lands, Europe and America, with huge Russia sitting astride both Europe and Asia, with a foot dangling on each side of the globe. For these, too, are mission lands. *Foreign*-mission lands, would you call them? Well, that depends entirely on what spot you happen to call home. They are all mission fields. The whole world is a mission field to God. *Foreign*-mission field? or *home*-mission? Which? It makes no practical matter which term you choose to use.

It will be well to remember just what that common phrase, "Christian lands," really means. It may help us in our praying. And it may help us, too, to keep humble as we think about heathen lands. It means, of course, the lands where Christian standards are commonly recognized as the proper standards of morals and of life.

It does *not* mean that the people are all Christian. Only a minority so class themselves; the great majority do not. Neither does it mean that that minority called Christian is *controlled* in daily life and in business by the principles of Jesus. For by pretty general consent they are not so controlled. It is not too much to say that there is more of that same spirit of selfishness that marks the heathen world, dominating the personal lives of people in Christian lands, than there is of the unselfish Christ spirit. That may sound unkind and too critical to you. It is not said in a critical spirit, but simply in the desire to get the facts as they are. I am fully persuaded that the more you think about it the more you will come to see that this is simply the truth.

Nor yet does that term, "Christian lands," mean that these lands are as distinctly Christian through and through as heathen lands are distinctly heathen, or non-Christian, through and through. As a matter of fact, Christian lands are not dominated as thoroughly by the Christian

The Need

spirit as heathen lands are by the heathen spirit. We really don't deserve our distinctive phrase as much as they deserve theirs.

It does mean chiefly this, that here in these lands the Christian Church has its stronghold; that Christian standards are commonly recognized, though in practice they are so commonly disregarded. It means that the enormous incidental blessings, in material and mental life, that always follow the preaching of the Gospel are here enjoyed most fully. And it means, too, that much of the humanizing, softening, and energizing power of the Gospel of Christ has seeped and soaked into our common civilization and affected all our life.

This is true; yet the mass of persons living in this atmosphere, and enjoying its great advantages, are wholly selfish in the main drive of their lives, and so in being selfish are un-Christian. While Christian ideals dominate so much of our life, the term "Christian lands" really describes our *privileges* more than it does our *practices*.

The Greatest Need.

A word now about these great Christian lands of Europe and America. The Catholic countries of Europe have been regarded as mission fields by the Protestant churches, and missionary operations have been conducted in them for many years. Russia has likewise been commonly regarded as missionary territory, and a very difficult one at that. In portions of Great Britain, in our own

Western States and frontiers, in the Southern mountain States, and in other sections, and among special classes, missionary work has been regularly carried on.

And the cities, those great, strange, throbbing hearts of human life, are all peculiarly mission fields. It is remarkable how the modern city reproduces world conditions morally. The city is a sort of miniature of the world. All the varying moral conditions of the heathen world, atheism, savagery almost, crude heathenish superstition, degradation of woman, neglect of children, and untempered lust, may be found in New York and Chicago, in London and Paris, in Vienna and Berlin, and in varying degree in all cities of Christian lands. The grosser parts are hidden away, more or less.

These conditions are softened in intensity by the commonly recognized moral standards of life. But they are there. The man immersed in mission service in any of these cities is apt to think that there can be no greater nor sorer need than this that pushes itself insistently upon him at every turn.

The slum ends and sides of our Christian cities and huge heathendom, jostle elbows in the likeness of their moral conditions. The need is everywhere, crying earnestly, wretchedly out to us. There is good mission ground anywhere you please to strike in.

But—*but*, by far the greatest need, with that word "greatest" intensified beyond all power of

The Need

description, is in the heathen lands. The vastness of the numbers there, the utter ignorance, the smallness of their chance of getting any of the knowledge and uplift of the Gospel, all go to spell out that word "greatest." The awful cumulative power of sin, unchecked by the common moral standards of life, with the terrific momentum of centuries; the common temptations known to us, but with a fierceness and subtlety wholly unknown to us in Christian lands—and yet how terrifically fierce and cunningly subtle some of us know them to be!—these all make every letter in that word "greatest" stand out in biggest capitals, and in blackest, inkiest ink.

Groping in the Dark.

That is a bare suggestion of the need of the world *in bulk*. But we want to get a much closer look than that. These are *men* that we are talking about; our *brothers*, not merely hard, unfeeling, statistical totals of millions. Each man of them contains the whole pitiable picture of the sore need of the world vividly portrayed in himself.

The very heathen religions themselves are the crying out, in the night, of men's hearts, after something they haven't, and yet need so much. Strange things these heathen superstitions and monstrous practices and beliefs called religions! It has been rather the thing of late to speak somewhat respectfully of them, and rather apologetically. They have even been praised, so strangely do things get mixed up in this world of ours. It has been supposed that God was revealing Himself in these religions; and that in them men were reaching up to God, and *could* reach up to Him through them.

They really are the twilight remnants of the clear direct light of God that once lightened all men; *but* so mixed through, and covered up with error and superstition and unnatural devilish lust, that they are wholly inadequate to lead any man back home to God. In almost all of them there is indeed some distinct kernel of truth. But that kernel has been invariably shut up in a shell and bur that are hard beyond any power of cracking, to get at the kernel of truth for practical help, even if the people knew enough to try.

They tell pathetically of the groping of man's heart after God. But the groping is in the pitch dark, and amid a mass of foul, filthy cobwebs that blind the eyes with their dust, and grime all the life. I have no doubt that untold numbers of true hearts in heathen lands are feeling after God, and in some dim way coming into touch with Him. He is not far from any one of them; but they find Him chiefly in spite of these religions, rather than through any help found in them.

The story is told of a Chinese tailor who had struggled hopelessly for light, and had finally found it in finding Jesus. He put his idea of the heathen religions that he knew, and had tried, in this simple vivid way:

The Need

"A man had fallen into a deep, dark pit, and lay in its miry bottom, groaning and utterly unable to move. He heard a man walking by close enough to see his plight. But with stately tread he walked on without volunteering to help. That is Mohammedanism.

"Confucius walking by approached the edge of the pit, and said, 'Poor fellow! I am sorry for you. Why were you such a fool as to get in there? Let me give you a piece of advice: If ever you get out, don't get in again.' 'I can't get out,' said the man. That is Confucianism.

"A Buddhist priest next came by and said: 'Poor fellow! I am very much pained to see you there. I think if you could scramble up two-thirds of the way, or even half, I could reach you and lift you up the rest.' But the man in the pit was entirely helpless and unable to rise. That is Buddhism.

"Next the Saviour came by, and, hearing his cries, went to the very brink of the pit, stretched down and laid hold of the poor man, brought him up, and said, 'Go, sin no more.' This is Christianity."

The awful moral or immoral conditions prevalent throughout the heathen world are the most graphic comment on the influence of these religions. It can be said thoughtfully that, instead of ever helping up to God and the light, they drag down to the devil and to black darkness. There is not only an utter lack of any moral uplift in them, but a deadly downward pull. The very things called religions point out piteously the terrible need of these peoples.

Living Messages of Jesus.

Now, what is it that these people need, and that we can give to them? May I first remind you what they don't need? Well, let it be said as plainly as it can be that they don't need the transferring to heathen soil of our Western church systems, nor our schemes of organizations. It is not our Western creeds and theology that they stand in need of.

Of course, there need to be both churches and organizations. Only so will the work be done, and what is gotten held together. But these are in themselves temporary. They are immensely important and indispensable, but not the chief thing. The great need is of *the story of Jesus*. That is, plain teaching about sin—the hardest task of all for the missionary, whether in Asia or America—and the damnable results locked up in sin. Then the winsome telling, the tirelessly patient and persistently gentle telling of the story of love, God's love as revealed in Jesus. The telling them that Jesus will put a new moral power inside a man that will make him over new.

But they need even more than this, aye, far more. They need *men*—human beings like themselves, living among them in closest touch—whose clean, strong, sweet lives spell out the Jesus-story as no human lips can ever tell it.

To live side by side with men who like them-

The Need

selves are tempted sorely, but who show plainly in their lives a power that downs the temptation— this is their great need. The good seed, after all, is not the message of truth merely, but the "sons of the kingdom," [1] men living the message of Jesus, and more, the power of Jesus, daily.

A kindergarten teacher opened a mission among the slum children of a very poor section of Chicago. She began her work by gathering a number of dirty, unkempt children of the street into the neat mission room. Then, instead of preaching or praying or something of the conventional sort at the first, she brought in and set on a table a large beautiful calla lily, bewitching in its simple white beauty.

The effect of the flower on one child, a little girl, was striking. No sooner had she looked at it than she looked down at her own dirty hands and clothes, with a flush creeping into her face. Then she quickly went out into the street. In a little while she was back again, but with her face washed, her hair combed, her dress tidied up, and a bit of colored ribbon added. She walked straight up to the lily again, and looked long, with deep wondering admiration in her eyes, at the beautiful white flower.

The flower's purity was a mirror in which she saw her own dirtiness. It was a magnet drawing her gently but strongly up to its own higher level. It was an inspiration moving her irresistibly to respond to its own upward pull.

[1] Matthew 13:38.

A simple, pure, human life is the greatest moral magnet. Jesus Himself down here was just such a magnet. Such a life is impossible for us without Jesus. It tells His power as no tongue can. It spells out loudly a standard of life and, far more, a power that can lift the life up to the standard. It doesn't simply tell what we should be. That may only tantalize and tease. But it tells what we actually can be.

Jesus is more than a message. He is a living power in a man's life. This is the great need of men's hearts,—the message of Jesus' purity and of Jesus' power *embodied in live men*, living side by side, in the thick of things, with their brothers of the great world.

The Great Unknown Lack.

The greatness of men's need stands out most pathetically in this, that men don't know their need. They have gotten so used to the night that they don't care for the sunlight. They have been hungry so long that the sense of hunger and the call of appetite have wholly gone.

There is a simple, striking story told of two famous Scandinavians, Ole Bull, the great violinist, and John Ericsson, the great inventor, who taught the world to use the screw in steam navigation. The one was a Norwegian, the other a Swede. They had been friends in early life, but drifted apart and did not meet again until each had become famous. The old friendship was renewed on one of Ole Bull's tours to this country.

The Need

As Bull was leaving his friend, after a delightful visit, he gave him a cordial invitation to attend his concert that evening. But the matter-of-fact, prosaic Ericsson declined, pleading pressure of work, and saying that he had no time to waste on music.

Bull renewed his invitation, time and again, finally saying, "If you won't come, I'll bring my violin down here to your shop, and play." "If you do," replied the famous engineer laughingly, "I'll smash the thing to pieces." The violinist, knowing the marvellous, almost supernatural, power of his instrument to touch and awaken the human heart into new life, felt curious to know what effect it would have on this scientific man steeped in his prosaic physics. So he planned a bit of diplomacy.

Taking the violin with him, he called upon Ericsson at his workshop one day. He removed the strings and screws and apron, and called Ericsson's attention to certain defects, asking about the scientific and acoustic principles involved, and discussing the differing effect of the different grain of certain woods. From this he went on to a discussion of sound waves. Finally, to illustrate his meaning and his questions, he replaced the parts, and, bringing the bow softly down upon the tense strings, drew out a few marvellously sweet, rich tones.

At once the workmen in the shop dropped their tools, and listened with wide-eyed wonder. Ole Bull played on and on, with his simple great skill, making the workshop a place of worship. When finally he paused, Ericsson lifted his bowed head, and showed eyes that were wet. Then he said softly, with the touch of reverent awe in his voice, "Play on! Don't stop. Play on. *I never knew before what it was that was lacking in my life.*"

That is what men everywhere say when they come to know Jesus. They fight against knowing Him because of their ignorance of Him. At home, prejudice against theology of this sort and that; against some preaching, or church service, or some Christian people they have unpleasant memories of perhaps, bar the way. Abroad, prejudice against their treatment at the hands of Christian nations, or against anything new, shuts the door with a slam and a sharp push of the bolt.

It takes great diplomacy, love's diplomacy, the combination of serpent and dove, subtlety and harmlessness, to get an entrance. But when the door is pried open, or coaxed open enough for some sound or sight of Jesus to get in, they passionately cry out, "This is what I need. This Jesus is the lacking thing in my life!"

THE PRESENT OPPORTUNITY

Somebody's Knocking at the Door.
They're Standing in the Dark.
Who's There?
The Coming Leaders.
What They're After.
Returning Our Call.
"Inasmuch."

The Present Opportunity

Somebody's Knocking at the Door.

THERE'S a soft, tender passion in the heart of God. Its flame burns steadily. It never flags nor dims. It's a passion for His child-man. And that very passion itself draws man to Himself with a drawing power that is irresistible. They can't resist being drawn, even though they may refuse to yield to it.

There is an answering passion in man's heart for God. It is often a sort of dumb longing, not clearly defined nor well understood. It is a mute yearning of his heart for God, though often he doesn't think of it that way. But it is there; for these two, man and God, belong together. They were together until sin drove its ugly wedge in between. They are a part of each other. Neither one is complete nor happy without the other.

The heart of God can be satisfied only as man comes back home to Him. And man's heart never rests until it finds rest in comradeship with God. These two are always drawing toward each other. God is always drawing man by the great master-passion of His heart. And man is always responding to that tender, strong pull in the underneath, mute yearning of his heart.

By and by the thing that keeps them apart will be gotten rid of. Sin will be shipped overboard, to fall by its own dead weight to the bottom of the sea. Then there will be glad reunion of God and man, their hearts in full glad accord again. To-night we want to talk together a bit about this answering passion of man's heart for God.

The heathen world is knocking to-day at the door of the Christian Church. It has found out who has the fullest and truest information about God. And it is knocking loudly and earnestly at that door. And it keeps on knocking, though the door seems to be barely open yet; and a good many—most?—inside don't seem to have heard the knocking.

The most remarkable thing about the present time from the Church point of view is that the heathen peoples are asking for what the Master has told us to give them. The centre of Church attraction and of Christian action to-day is on the swing toward heathen lands.

When the Church began again, a hundred years ago, to enter the great heathen world, it had to use pick and axe, jimmy and chisel. It seemed like using burglar's tools. Certainly it was working in the dark, with only the burglar's dark-lantern to show the way. But now the heathen door is wide open. Instead of our knocking at their door, the heathen world is knocking at our door.

Our billion brothers stand in the night-time

The Present Opportunity

of their darkness blindly feeling for our door, and knocking, now timidly, now earnestly and loudly, ay, imperiously, for the light that we have. It has been a cold night for them, and a long night, too. But the darkest hour of it is already throbbing with the flood of coming light. They have found the door and are using it. The whole foreign non-Christian world is knocking with incessant, insistent clamor at our church door.

They're Standing in the Dark.

I do not mean that actually every country in the world is open to the Gospel. For there are a few countries with comparatively scanty populations that are not open; except, indeed, on the edges, to the man prying earnestly around for a way to get in.

I don't mean that every man in these open countries is actually asking us to send him some word of Jesus. For vast numbers of them have never heard either about us or about Him. They don't know there is a Jesus to ask about; or, judging by others, they would be asking.

Neither do I mean that these multitudes who are asking are, in every case, asking for the Gospel itself. For many times that is not so. They ask for that which appeals to them strongly as something that they want. They want our Western science and learning. They want to get from us the secret of harnessing nature up to their wagon to pull their heavy loads.

In many cases, without doubt, they don't

want our Christianity at all. They regard it simply as something that goes along inseparably with the thing they do want. They are willing to put up with some of it for a while, if only they can get the thing they are after. Their eyes have been caught by the bright light of our Christian civilization. They don't understand how it came to us. They haven't wakened up enough, most of them, to think into that.

They want the light we have, as we might want something that we could order a shipment of. They haven't learned enough yet to want to get the light-generating plant installed in their midst. The great fact that all our civilization has come to us through the partial presence of the Light of the world hasn't dawned upon their minds yet.

But, however selfish motives and a crude understanding or misunderstanding may enter in, the great strange unprecedented fact still remains true that the world of heathenism is knocking at the door of Christendom as never before in the world's history.

And then, too, everywhere some of them are asking plainly and piteously for the real thing. Great numbers in all the foreign-mission lands are asking that Christian teachers be sent to them with Bibles and other books to teach them the way back home to God. Wherever they find out that there is a knowledge of God to be gotten, from there comes the insistent knocking that it be brought to them.

The Present Opportunity

I remember Bishop Bashford, of the Methodist Episcopal Church, stationed in China, telling of one of his thrilling experiences out there. He had gone inland quite a bit into China on one of his tours. One day he was preaching the story of Jesus to a crowd of Chinese gathered in the open air. As his interpreter turned his words into Chinese the crowds listened with great respect and keenest interest.

As he finished he asked them if they had ever heard the Gospel before. No; none of them had. He was turning up absolutely fresh soil. And they pressed in about him, earnestly asking that men be sent to tell them. And this experience of Bishop Bashford's is being repeated, over and over again, throughout the foreign-mission world.

Who's There?

But there is yet more than this. Everywhere among these peoples, as one comes into close enough touch to find their hearts, there can be found underneath the inarticulate, inexpressible yearning for something they haven't. And they don't know enough to know what it is they long for. But they are conscious of the constant, weary, yearning tug within. The great heart of the non-Christian world to-day is asking dumbly, but earnestly, as only the heart can ask, for the light we have. Its knocking at our front door is growing louder in its insistent earnestness.

Since Commodore Perry steamed into the harbor of Yokohama, fifty years ago, with open

Bible and American flag, and knocked at the front door of the Orient, the whole situation has completely changed. Then we knocked for admission to these shut-in lands. Now they are knocking at our door, for the knowledge and light that we have in Christian lands because we have Jesus.

May I call your attention to some of the louder of these knockings?

For years students in great numbers, thousands, have been coming from these heathen nations to our country to get our Western learning. Throughout the colleges and lower schools of the land, both East and West, in the greater universities, and in the more modest small church colleges they can be found.

I remember a sight that never failed to thrill me in my visitations among the colleges of our Central West. Almost always I saw one or more of these young men, from Japan, and less frequently from China and India and other countries, and sometimes young women, too, studying in these institutions. Quite frequently they came from the better families of their people; often from old wealthy families of position and influence. So that by blood ties and position they will be the future men of influence and leaders of their people. And it is a notable fact that many of them are to-day the leaders in Japan. Literally thousands of them have come, these thousands of miles around the world, to knock at our doors, and ask for what we have and they haven't.

Even more striking is the recent visitation to us of official commissions from the non-Christian lands. One after another, these national governmental deputations have come to us. They have been composed of the strongest men in these lands, men in leading official position. They have come by government appointment, and at government expense, to learn the secret of our marvellous Western progress.

And in addition to these official deputations others have come, men of like prominence and influence, coming on their own account, to witness our civilization and learn its secrets.

The Coming Great Leaders.

One of the most remarkable incidents of this most remarkable movement has been the great migration of young Chinese men to study in the colleges of Japan. Within a very short space of time, as though by a concerted movement, fifteen thousand Chinese young men have flocked to Tokyo. The inevitable sifting process has sent many back, but fully ten thousand remain, engaged in earnest, hard study.

Will you mark very keenly why they went to *Japan?* Because to them Japan, in its new life, stood for the new light and life of the West. Their little, but mighty, aggressive neighbor on their eastern shore had brought to their very door the new civilization of the Christian West.

Here was an unusual opportunity. Where hundreds had come clear around the earth to us, thousands have seized this opportunity close at hand. They come from every province of China; even that farthest away, on the border of Tibet, sending hundreds.

The travel involved thousands of miles. And if their slow means of travel be taken into account, it meant what would be to us practically hundreds of thousands of miles. Hundreds of them have been sent by the provincial and local governments. Others have come through private funds made up for the purpose. And wealthy men have sent their sons. They have gone to Japan only because Japan has opened her doors so widely to our Christian civilization. It is not to their conqueror, Japan, they have come, but to the civilization which Japan has imported from Christian lands.

Was there ever such a knocking at the door of the Christian Church as this? Ten thousand picked men, of the best and keenest young manhood of China, representing all parts of the empire, and in large part representing the government, settling down to years of close study of our Christian civilization as found in Japan— a tremendous fact for the Church to-day! Things are crowding in on us. It is the non-Christian world knocking at our back door. It was too far around to the front. So they have commenced their knocking at the nearest and handiest door they could find.

Then there are direct requests coming constantly to the missionaries, from the peoples in all these

The Present Opportunity 91

lands, earnestly asking and even pleading that men be sent to teach them of God and of Christ. Whole villages have been found in the fastnesses of Africa's wilds spending days together, and all day long, on their knees in prayer; most often mute prayer with upturned faces—their very bent bodies their prayer—that news of the white man's God might be sent to them.

In Korea and other lands it is no uncommon thing for men and women to travel hundreds of miles by their slow transportation, or even to come a-foot, to attend gatherings where the story of Jesus is being preached.

And then, too, there is the indirect knocking in the imitation of our Western ways, and throwing away of their own. Imitation is the highest form of compliment that can be paid. It tells of admiration, and of a desire to be as those imitated. The adapting of Western learning by these conservative Oriental peoples, the establishment of thousands of colleges and schools on the model of Christian countries is so radical a thing as to be nothing short of startling. The abandoning of bad customs, as well as of their old systems of education, is as startling. Where there were antagonisms there is now the friendliest imitation.

If to this we add the remarkable immigration to our shores, of a million a year, it intensifies enormously the opportunity of service brought to us by foreign peoples. Yet please notice that this latter is not Asia nor Africa coming to us, but Europe.

However crying their need may be, these are, nominally, not heathen peoples, but chiefly from Christianized Europe. The Asiatics would have come in great numbers, but that door was promptly shut and carefully locked by official hands.

As you swing your eye over these seething masses of the heathen world, and listen to their voices, let me ask you, with the earnest softness of tone that belongs to the heart, could there be a louder knocking at the door of the Christian Church?

What Do They Want?

There can be no doubt about the knocking. But—*but* what is it they are after? Well, in plainest talk, they are after the thing that has made Christian nations great, great to the point of world-leadership and world-supremacy.

Do you remember the famous reply, often quoted, given to a foreign visitor at the English court? He had asked the secret of the greatness of England, which impressed him so forcibly. And her gracious majesty, of blessed memory, Queen Victoria, placed her hand upon a Bible, and replied in the memorable words, "*This* is the secret of England's greatness."

Just how much that wise woman had in mind I am sure I do not know. I feel very sure she did not refer to the church system of England. But to something far more and deeper than that, of which the church system is only one expression.

The Present Opportunity

Where the Bible has gone, and where it has so largely dominated the life of the people, as in England, there has been both a moral regeneration *and*, mark it keenly, a *new mental life*. Its touch has awakened the mental powers. There has been aroused and released into activity that *spirit of energy* which has become the most marked characteristic of the Western world.

These two, the mental life and the remarkable energy, lie at the basis of all our wonderful modern science. And this, in turn, lies at the basis of all our phenomenal development. It is this that makes the West different from the East. The leading nations are Christian nations. The germ of vigorous life is in the Gospel of Christ.

This is the thing the heathen world is knocking so earnestly at our door for to-day. I do not say that they think of it in that way. They are just coming, groping out of the darkness, with eyes blinking and blinded by the brightness of our light. They stretch eager, reaching fingers out toward the light, without knowing much about it. The glare of it has caught them.

And if they are caught, moth-like, and hurt by its flame—if they copy our vile vices, which are no part of our Christianity, but the remnants of our own original savagery cropping out in spite of Christianity—if so, is it surprising? Their eyes are bothered by the sudden change from black darkness to brilliant light.

But there's a deeper asking. Underneath all, the thing they are really asking for, all unconsciously most of them, is that which lies at the root of all our Western progress. They ask unknowingly for the Gospel of Christ, the heart of this precious old Bible. When they get that they will find that it brings the new awakening of mental life and the new aggressive energy that has made us Christian nations what we are.

Returning Our Call.

Will you please remember that their knocking at our door is a direct result of our knocking at their door? They are very polite, these far-away kinsfolk of ours. They are simply returning our call.

The missionary, from Great Britain, and America, and Europe, has been the West's pathfinder in these foreign-mission lands. He has blazed a way into these thick woods, and beaten down narrow foot-paths through them. It's been hard, heroic work. The pathfinder has often gotten his hands and face badly torn by the thick brambly thorn bushes as he pushed resolutely on.

Then diplomacy entered and broadened the roads. And commerce quickly came and beat them down into good hard shape for easy travel. And in turn the missionaries have freely used the broader, better roads.

And now these roads are being trodden by other feet, and in an opposite direction. Along the pathways made by the Church, and made better by diplomacy and commerce, these peoples are coming, coming a-running, to ask us to give them

The Present Opportunity

what we have. We received it from Another. He bade us give it as freely as we received it.

Here they come eagerly knocking at our doors, front door, and back door, and wherever there is a door. Do you hear them?

Ah! The great question to-day is not a question for the heathen world, but for the Christian Church—shall we respond to the opportunity they are flinging in our faces? To-day there are more hands in heathen lands stretched out *for* the Gospel of Jesus than there are Christian hands stretched out *with* the Gospel. More hearts in those far-away lands are dumbly praying for the light than there are of us praying that they may receive the light—far more.

The greatest question for the Church to-day is—shall we enter the open door? And this is a key-question, too. Its answer includes a full satisfactory answer to all the other questions we are discussing. All questions of finance, of uncertain wabbling pulpit voices, of careless and indifferent or empty pews, and of city evangelization will quickly find an answer as the Church fully and faithfully answers this. Here is the work that, if done, and well done, will bring a new circulation of blood into the whole life of the Church.

Have you noticed the sharp contrast that there is gradually growing up between the way people at home and these foreign peoples are receiving the Gospel? Out there there is an openness to the truth, an eager willingness to believe it simply, and to act upon it, that suggests the way they did in the Book of Acts. In our home-lands of America and Great Britain and Germany there seems to be either indifference, or an atmosphere of quibble and criticism. With questions and doubts naturalistic explanations are sought that do away with much of the simple force of God's truth.

A like difference is showing itself between the results there and here. Here they are scantier, and gotten with great difficulty; there much larger, and with greater ease. There the door is wide-open, and people crowding in; here there is a feeling that the door is closing, surely and not slowly people turn away elsewhere. There has come to be an unusual proportion of pickles and salads and other relishes served with every spreading of the Gospel meal here. There, just plain unbuttered bread is eagerly and thankfully sought for. They are hungry. And their hunger is a wide-open door to us. We need the exercise of foreign travel, and a great deal of it, to bring back our zest.

"*Inasmuch.*"

May I speak very softly of another side of this knocking at our door? *Who* is it that is knocking? Aye, *Who* ?

Do you remember Jesus' words in Matthew, chapter twenty-five? He is speaking of the settling-up time that is to come at the close of things. And He does something there that is startling. He *identifies Himself* with the hungry and cold and poor. That is, He puts Himself in their place.

The Present Opportunity

They are reckoned as though they were He. He says that when they asked for some food and warm clothes *it was really Himself asking for food and warmth!* We have been really dealing with Him when we have met these needy ones. The one test question He makes for all is this—What did you do for these hungry people? Because what you did, or didn't do for them, was done or refused to *Me*. Jesus comes in the guise of the needy. Who is it knocking at our door so loudly to-day?

I suppose if you could think of Jesus actually coming to-day to New York, the human Jesus I mean, coming as a man just as He came to Jerusalem, but known to us as He is now—I suppose there is hardly a door that would not open to Him. He might not be any better understood in New York than He was in Jerusalem, but the doors of the wealthy would quickly open to Him. I mean the Christian wealthy, the Church wealthy; other doors, too, no doubt, but these surely. He would have a great welcome.

And I suppose, too, that if in some wealthy home on Fifth Avenue or Madison Avenue He were to ask His host to give some large sum, a million dollars or ten millions, for sending the Gospel to China or Japan His request would likely be granted. It seems to me rather probable that it would. Well, how can it be put plainly enough that He does come to our doors, rich, and less rich; and poor. He's at the front door now, knocking and asking our help.

In these heathen peoples of His, *Jesus* comes to us. And we have been giving Him—shall I say it very softly for sheer shame?—we have given, not all, but most of us, what is practically the loose change in our trousers' pocket; not actually, of course; sometimes even that. We have spent more on everything else. We have made up boxes of cast-off clothes and old shoes for—*Jesus!* This has been a large part of our answer. Is it any wonder the hot blood sends the color climbing into our cheeks at the thought, and that we instinctively seek for some explanation that will soften the hard rub of the truth!

I found a bit of a poem in a magazine some time ago that caught fire as I read it. It was written, I judge, in a personal sense; but it came to me at once with a wider meaning; and it persists in so coming at every reading of it.

In this poem there is some one knocking at a door for admission, and a voice without calls,

> "'Friend, open to *Me*.' Who is this that calls?
> Nay, I am deaf as are my walls;
> Cease crying, for I will not hear
> Thy cry of hope or fear.
> What art thou indeed
> That I should heed
> Thy lamentable need?
> Hungry, should feed,
> Or stranger, lodge thee here?"

But the voice persists—

> " 'Friend, My feet bleed.
> Open thy door to Me and comfort Me.'

"I will not open; trouble me no more.
Go on thy way footsore,
I will not arise and open unto thee.

And still the pleading,

" 'Then is it nothing to thee? Open, see
Who stands to plead with thee.
Open, lest I should pass thee by, and thou
One day entreat My face
And cry for grace,
And I be deaf as thou art now;
Open to Me.'

"Then I cried out upon him: Cease,
Leave me in peace;
Fear not that I should crave
Aught thou may'st have.
Leave me in peace, yea, trouble me no more,
Lest I arise and chase thee from my door.
What! shall I not be let
Alone, that thou dost vex me yet?

"But all night long that voice spake urgently—
'Open to Me.'
Still harping in mine ears—
'Rise, let Me in.'
Pleading with tears—
'Open to Me, that I may come to thee.'
While the dew dropp'd, while the dark hours
    were cold—
'My feet bleed, see My Face,
See My hands bleed that bring thee grace,
My heart doth bleed for thee—
Open to Me.'

"So, till the break of day;
Then died away
That voice, in silence as of sorrow;
Then footsteps echoing like a sigh

Pass'd me by;
Lingering footsteps, slow to pass.
On the morrow
I saw upon the grass
Each footprint mark'd in blood, and *on my door
The mark of blood forevermore.*" [1]

That same voice still comes with a strangely gentle persistence—

"Inasmuch as ye did it
Unto one of these my brethren, even these least,
Ye did it unto Me.

"Inasmuch as ye did it *not*
Unto one of these least,
Ye did it *not* unto Me."[2]

[1] Christina Rossetti, in *The Outlook*, slightly altered.
[2] Matthew 25:40, 45.

THE PRESSING EMERGENCY

The October Panic.
Danger and Victory Eying Each Other.
Spirit Contests.
A Westernized Heathenism.
A Crisis of Neglect and Success.
A Powerless Christianity.
Death or Deep Water.
Saved by Saving.

The Pressing Emergency

The October Panic.

A man walked up the steps of a well-known bank in lower New York one morning, about a half-hour before opening-time, and stood before the shut door. In a few minutes another came, and stood waiting beside him. Others came, one by one, until soon a small group stood in line, waiting for the door to open.

A messenger boy, coming down the street, quickly took in the unusual sight. He wasn't old enough to have been through any of New York's notable panics, and he had never witnessed a run on a bank; but quick as a flash, or as a Wall-Street messenger boy, he knew as though by instinct that a run was on at that bank. Instantly he started running down the street to tell others.

No prairie wild-fire ever spread so quickly as the news ran over 'phone wires of the beginning of that run. As though by some sort of invisible ether-waves, the news seemed to spread through the financial district. Every bank president seemed to know at once. Then it spread throughout the city, and the greater city.

So began what has been called the October

panic of last year, which quickly spread through the land, and then throughout the world until every country bank here, and every capital city abroad, felt the sharp tightening of the money-bag strings.

It was a strange panic. You couldn't just tell what was responsible for it. The very variety of explanations, editorial and other, told of the lack of a common understanding of what caused it. There had been no famine or drought. The crops, the chief financial barometer of the country's condition, had been remarkably abundant. There had been no overproduction or glutting of the industrial world. Indeed, great numbers of concerns had been embarrassed by orders that they couldn't fill fast enough. The cause seemed to be wholly in people's *minds*. A spirit of distrust of some of the great money leaders and of their methods was abroad. That feeling of fear sent a few men, by an unplanned concert of action, to a certain bank before ten o'clock one morning.

The unusual sight of a few men standing in line waiting for the opening of that bank door was like a lighted match to a barn full of dry hay. At the first inkling of a suggestion of a financial panic money began to disappear. Nothing is so cowardly in its cautiousness as money. Scholarship comes next to it. The savings of years have the tightest grip on most human hands. As though by magic, money began hunting dark holes in stockings and cellars and safety-deposit

The Pressing Emergency

boxes. And the hard grip of the panic was quickly felt everywhere. It was a fear panic. A terrible danger was at hand.

At once the regular habit of life was disturbed for great numbers of men. The Secretary of the Treasury quit his Washington desk and spent several days in New York so as to be able to give the help of the Government's funds and enormous prestige where they would count for most, and to give promptly. Bank officials and other financial leaders cut social engagements and everything else that could be cut, and devoted themselves to meeting the sudden emergency. They ate scantily, both to save time and for lack of appetite, and to help keep their heads clear for quick decisive thinking and action. The tension was intense. Men sat up all night conferring on best measures.

A group of the leading money men met in the private quarters of one of their numbers, about whose rugged personality and leadership they instinctively rallied. More than one night the gray dawning light of the morning found them, with white, drawn faces, still in conference. The emergency gripped them. An emergency always does. The habits of life are upset, helter-skelter, in the effort to avert the threatening danger. That was an emergency in the money world. Grave danger threatened. Everything else was forgotten, and every bit of available resource strained to turn the danger aside. It *was* turned aside. That was a splendid achievement. And even though men have been feeling the effects for this whole year, what they have felt is as nothing compared with what might have come.

Danger and Victory Eying each other.

An emergency means a great danger threatening, perhaps the very life. But it means, too, that if the danger can be gripped and overcome there will be great victory. Two possibilities come up close and stare each other angrily in the face; the possibility of great disaster impending, and of great victory over it within grasp, if there be a reaching hand to grasp it. The deciding thing is the human element, the strong, quick hand stretched out. If strength can be concentrated, the situation gripped, then great victory is assured. But it takes the utmost concentration of strength, with rare wisdom and quick steady action, to turn the tide toward flood. If this is not done, either because of lack of leadership or of enough strength or enough interest, disaster comes.

Just such emergencies come to us constantly. A severe illness lays its hand upon a loved one in the home. The crisis comes. Death and life stand in the sick-room eying each other. Either one may be victor. No one can tell surely which it will be. And every effort is strained, the habit of life broken, other matters forgotten and neglected, that death may be staved off, and life wooed to stay. And when the crisis passes safely the joy over the new lease of life makes one forget all the cost of strain and effort.

The Pressing Emergency

Who of us cannot recall some time back there, when some emergency came in personal business matters, and personal and home expenses and plans were cut down to the lowest notch, to the bleeding-point, that the emergency might be safely met.

Teachers and parents know that moral emergencies come at intervals in a child's life, until young manhood and womanhood are reached. One of the greatest tasks in child-training is to note the emergency, and meet it successfully. And what keenness and patience and subtlety it does take only he knows who has been through the experience.

Spirit Contests.

Emergencies come in spiritual matters, too. They are the hardest kind to meet. It is hardest to make people see them and grip them. In the life of many a church a spiritual emergency has come, but has not been met. The church goes on holding services, raising money and paying it out, going through all the proper forms, but with the life itself quite gone out of it. The thing is being kept in motion by a humanly manipulated electric current; there is no free life-movement.

Evangelistic leaders say that such emergencies come in their campaigning. There has to be a struggle of spirit forces. And the victory that comes, comes only as a result of close hand-to-hand conflict of soul by the leaders.

We all know that such crises come in our personal experience. And those who know about changing things by prayer do not need to be told of the emergency that comes at times; nor of how it requires a tightening of all the buckles, a new reviewing of the promises on which prayer rests, a new steadying of one's faith, a quietly persistent hanging on, an intenser insistence of spirit in prayer and more arrow-praying in the daily round of work —sending out the softly breathed heart-pleadings while busy with common duties, until the assurance comes that the danger is past and the victory secure.

It is remarkable to what an extent the great events of history have been emergency events. With the greatest reverence, it can be said that history's central event, the dying of Jesus, was an emergency action. Even though we understand clearly that it was known and counselled from before the foundation of the world, that He was to shed His precious blood for our salvation, His dying can never be fully understood save as a great emergency measure, *the* great emergency measure, because of the crisis made by sin.

Now that is the sort of thing—an emergency—that is now on in this great task of world-wide evangelization which Jesus has committed to our hands. Some of you may be strongly inclined to lift your eyebrows and ask—Is there really any such emergency? I know that people don't like those words "crisis" and "emergency." It is much more comfortable to think that things are going on very smoothly and well. Even though all is not

The Pressing Emergency

just as we might choose to have it, yet we like to think that it will turn out well. There is a sort of optimism that is very popular. Things will all come out right somehow, we like to think. But the fact is that things don't turn out right of themselves. They have to be turned by somebody who gives heart and life to the turning.

It can be said with sane, sober sense that without doubt there is an emergency, and a great one, in this foreign-mission enterprise. It is, of course, true that in a sense there is *a continual emergency* here. There are thousands of these foreign brothers of ours slipping the tether of life daily. The light might easily have been taken to them, and have changed their choices. But then it hasn't been, and the dark shadow of the possibility of their separating themselves forever from God, through wrong choice persisted in, hangs down over each one of them. There can be no darker shadow except the actual knowledge that they have so separated themselves from life in Him.

A Crisis of Neglect and Success.

But quite distinct from that, and in addition to it, it is quite safe to say that there is *an emergency now on* in the heathen world such as it has never known before. Such is the mature judgment of our missionary leaders.

And we do well to remind ourselves that we have some remarkable men among these leaders. There are men on the foreign fields and at the missionary helm at home of most remarkable ability and genius. There are to-day men of statesmanlike grasp and power, who could easily have taken front rank in public life, in diplomacy, and professional life, men fully able to fill the Presidential chair and do it masterfully, who are giving their life-blood to this great missionary task.

The sober judgment of these men, taken from every angle of vision, is that the present is a time of unparalleled emergency. It exists peculiarly in Asia, the greatest of all foreign-mission lands. It has been caused by a number of things that now come together with such force as to make a crisis, *the* crisis of missions, the gravest that has yet come, and that, it is probably safe to say, will ever come. For the future will be largely settled, one way or the other, within a few years.

At the basis of all is *the great need*, of course. That looms big and gaunt and spectral in any survey of the matter.

Then *the neglect* by the Church for many generations has greatly intensified the present situation. The Master's plan plainly is that every generation of the Church shall give the Gospel to its generation; that is, to all the people living in the world at that time. Every generation of men must have the Gospel afresh. No land is beyond the need of a fresh gospelizing. If Christian America were to lose its churches and the Gospel, it would surely revert to the heathen type from which we sprung.

But many generations went by with practically

The Pressing Emergency

nothing of this sort being done. These generations of inactivity have piled up on the present generation. The undone work of the past adds greatly to the task of the present. The present situation is abnormal because of what hasn't been done.

Then *the success of the present* has played a big part. Modern missionary activity has had a big share in making this emergency. A century of missions is reaching a tremendous climax. The splendid aggressiveness of church leaders and missionaries is now an embarrassment to a Church, or any one in the Church, who doesn't want to keep up the pace. It is an emergency of success, the logical result of what has been accomplished. So much has been done, and been done so well by a comparatively few, that now more must be done by the rest of us.

It's because the heathen world is awake that there is an emergency. Their awakeness is the thing that crowds in on us. And we waked them up. We must now do more and better, because we have done so well. We have indeed waked them up, but—to what? A business man would stamp it as rank foolishness to fail to take advantage of the splendid opening that we have made in the foreign-mission world.

A Westernized Heathenism.

Now, let us look just a bit at this present pressing emergency. There are grave perils threatening, and a great victory possible.

Well, first of all there is real danger of *a new aggressive heathenism;* a new, energetic, but distinctly un-Christian civilization in the heathen world. Many thoughtful men who are keenly watching the world movement believe that without doubt there is to be a new leadership of the human race in the Orient. It *may* be a heathen leadership. That danger is a distinct possibility. The new world-leadership may have all the enormous energy and mental keenness of Christian peoples, but without the Christian spirit.

That means practically a new heathenism, no longer asleep but wide-awake; no longer being manipulated by the Western nations, but maybe manipulating and managing them. An aroused, organized, energized heathen world, with all the science and inventiveness and restless aggressiveness of the western nations and, mark you—*and* all the spirit of the old, Godless, Christless heathenism dominating its new life—that is the danger.

The heathen world is awake at last after a sleep of centuries. It is sitting up, rubbing its eyes, and taking notice. It is entering upon a new life. That's as clear as a sunbeam on a cloudless morning. What that life shall be depends entirely on the Church waking up. That means, to be more practical, that it depends on you and me waking up, just now, and doing what we easily can. It *may* be a new *Christian* life, shot through and through with the blessed principles and spirit of Jesus. It *may* be a new life of energized, Western-

The Pressing Emergency 113

ized heathenism! They may get merely our energy and mental awakeness without the Christian spirit that gave these to us.

These two opposite things are standing by the bedside eying each other. Which will get the patient? Who knows? If the Church fail——! This is a real peril seriously threatening. It is probably far more grave and far more likely than the best-informed and keenest observer is aware of.

A Powerless Christianity.

Then there is a second danger climbing in fast on the heels of this, that is already being plainly felt. *These peoples may turn away from a Christianity that seems powerless to them.* As they come to know better the simple principles of our faith they may see that we are not true to it. Our Master bade us go everywhere and tell all men of Him, and tell them most and best by the way we live. But we haven't done it. The Church of the past nineteen centuries, taken as a whole, hasn't done it. The Church to-day, taken as a whole, isn't doing it.

How many times have the missionaries been obliged to listen to the question, which is a reproach rather than a question, "Why didn't you come before? My father lived and died in distress, seeking for this light you bring us now. *Why didn't your father come and tell my father?*" If they find that our faith hasn't gripped *us* enough to master our lives they will naturally doubt if, after all, there is any more real practical power in it than in their own heathen beliefs.

It *seems* better in theory, but it seems to lose its ideals in the stiff test of practice. They would be wrong in thinking that, of course. But what conclusion more natural to the crowd that never thinks deep. When all the difficulties and hardships come in the way of their acceptance of Christ, and the easiest way is not to, how easy to throw the whole thing aside.

The story is told of a Chinaman in this country who applied for a position as house-servant in a family which belonged to a fashionable church. He was asked:

"Do you drink whiskey?"

"No, I Clistian man."

"Do you play cards?"

"No, I Clistian man."

He was engaged, and proved to be a capable servant. By and by the lady gave a bridge-party, with wine accompaniments. The Chinaman did his part acceptably, but the next morning he appeared before his mistress.

"I want quit," he said.

"Why? What is the matter?"

"I Clistian man. I told you so before; no heathen; no workee for 'Melican heathen."

These heathen brothers of ours are not fools. They are a keen lot. They judge our religion by us who profess it, as we do with them and theirs. There may come a wide-spread practical disbelief, or lack of belief, that there is any practical

The Pressing Emergency

power in Christ to change a man's life, and really control his actions. And it will be a perfectly logical conclusion from what they find in us Christian nations as a whole.

Death or Deep Water.

And then there are some mighty bad dangers on the other side—*our* side. If it be true that every generation *needs* the Gospel, it is just as true that every generation of Christians *needs to give* the Gospel. It is the very life of a Christian to give himself out in earnest service for others. The man who is failing there has started on the down grade in his Christian life. If we lose the spirit of "go" we have lost the very Christian spirit itself. A disobedient church will become a dead church. It will die of heart failure.

It was John's Man with eyes of searching flame, and tongue of keen-edged sword, and feet that had been through the fire, who said to a Christian church, "I will move thy candlestick out of its place except thou change thy ways."[1] The candlestick isn't the light. It holds the light. The Church's great mission is to be the world's light-holder.

But unsnuffed candles and cobwebby window-panes seem to have been in evidence sometimes. The Christian Church in some lands has plainly lost its privilege of service, and lost its life, too. The old organizations are kept up, but all life has gone. There's a grave danger threatening

[1] Revelation 2:5.

the American Church and the British Church just at this present time.

Long years ago, in the days before steam navigation, an ocean vessel came from a long sea voyage, up St. George's Channel, headed for Liverpool. When the pilot was taken on board, he cried abruptly to the captain, "What do you mean? You've let her drift off toward the Welsh coast, toward the shallows. Muster the crew." The crew was quickly mustered, and the pilot told the danger in a few short words, and then said sharply, "Boys, it's death or deep water, hoist the mains'l!" And only by dint of hardest work was the ship saved.

If I could get the ear of the Church to-day, I would, as a great kindness to it, cry out with all the earnestness of soul I could command, "*It's death or deep water;* deep water in this holy service of world-winning, or death from foundering."

Saved by Saving.

And then there's a yet graver peril threatening. It's quite the common thing to appeal to selfish motives. It is striking that the great strides that prohibition has made of recent years, have been due to a sort of legislation and to business regulation that appeal to selfish motives. The economic motive, and the disagreeable and injurious likelihood of a saloon being close to one's own home, have had greater influence than higher moral motives. And we are glad of any motive that will put the damnable traffic down and out.

The Pressing Emergency

Well, I'm going to come down a step here, and remind you of a yet graver peril that threatens. There is serious danger of *a heathenized Christianity* dominating our boasted Christian civilization and Christian lands. And in time that would be a serious menace to our pocket-books.

That is to say, there may be the energy and keen mental life without the mellowing and sweetening influence of the Christian spirit. The restless aggressiveness may come without the poise; the ceaseless activity without the deeper steadying quality; the keenness without the softening touch of the true life. In other words, if we don't Christianize heathendom, they will exert an influence on us that will practically amount to their heathenizing Christendom.

Already such influences are seeping in at more than one crack. Mohammedanism has an active propaganda in Great Britain. Heathen wedges are slipping their thin edges in, in our land. More and more it will extend, in time influencing our whole moral fabric, and affecting our whole national life.

During some recent researches among the ruins of Pompeii the explorers turned up a find that told its own story. It was the body of a crippled boy. He was lame in his foot. And around the body there was a woman's arm, a finely shaped, beautiful, bejewelled arm. The mute find told its simple story. The great stream of fire suddenly coming from the volcano, the crowd fleeing for life, the little cripple unable to get along fast enough, the woman's heart touched, her arm thrown about the boy to aid his escape; then the overtaking fire-flood, and both lost. The arm that was stretched out to save another was preserved, and only that. All the rest of the brave rescuer's body had gone. The saving part was saved. Only that mercifully outstretched to save another was itself saved.

The Church or the man that selfishly saveth his life shall lose it. He that forgetteth about his own life in eagerly saving others shall find that he has saved his own life, and that it has grown into a new fulness and richness of life.

These are some of the dark ugly faces peering into ours. But there's another face among them. It is a very bright face, with eyes all aglow, and features all shining with light. It is the face of victory over every danger and difficulty that threatens. Many believe that the emergency will be met. The victory will surely be achieved. But the fact to mark keenly, just now, is that it will be achieved only by a vigorous, masterful gripping of the present pressing emergency.

Ah! God, may Thy Church—we men who make Thy Church, who *are* Thy Church—may we see the emergency, and be gripped by it; for Jesus' sake; aye, for men's sake; for the Church's sake; for our own sake; in Jesus' great name.

THE PAST FAILURE

Some of God's Failures.
Where the Reproach of Failure Lies.
God's Sovereignty.
The Church Mission.
"Christ also Waits."
"Somebody Forgets."

The Past Failure

Some of God's Failures.

GOD fails, sometimes. That is to say, the plan He has made and set His heart upon fails.

Eden was God's plan for man. A weedless, thornless, world-garden of great beauty and fruitfulness; a man and woman living together in sweet purity and strong self-mastery; their children growing up in such an atmosphere, trained for the highest and best; the earth with all its wondrous forces developed and mastered by man; full comradeship and partnership between man and all the living creation, beast and bird; and in the midst of all God Himself walking and working in closest touch with man in all his enterprises—that was God's Eden plan for man. But it failed.

The Israel plan was a failure, too. The main purpose of Israel being made God's peculiar people has failed up to the present hour. That plan originally was a simple shepherd people, living on the soil close to nature. They were to be, not a democracy ruled by the direct vote of the people in all things; nor a republic ruled by the vote of selected representatives; nor yet a kingdom ruled over by the will of an autocrat; but something quite distinct from all of these, what men have been pleased to call a theocracy.

That is to say, God Himself was to be their ruler in a very real, practical sense, directing and working with them in the working out of all their national life. They were to combine all the best in each of these forms of government, with a something added, not in any of them as men know them.

They were to be wholly unlike the other nations, utterly unambitious politically, neither exciting war upon themselves by others nor ever making war upon others. Their great mission was to be a teacher-nation to all the earth, teaching the great spiritual truths; and, better yet, embodying these truths in their personal and national life.

But the plan failed. The glitter of the other nations turned them aside from God's plan. They set up a kingdom, "like all the nations," very much like them.

Then God worked with them where they would work with Him. He planned a great kingdom to overspread the earth in its rule and blessed influence, but not by the aggression of war and oppression. Their later literature is all a-flood with the glory light of the coming king and kingdom. Yet when the King came they rejected Him and then killed Him. They failed at the very point that was to have been their great achievement. God's plan failed. The Hebrew people from the point of view of the direct object of

The Past Failure

their creation as a nation have been a failure up to the present hour.

God's choice for their first king, Saul, was a failure, too. No man ever began life, nor king his rule, with better preparation and prospects. And no career ever ended in such dismal failure. God's plan for the man had failed.

Jesus' plan for Judas failed. The sharpest contrasts of possible good and actual bad came together in his career in the most startling way. He failed at the very point where he should have been strongest—his personal loyalty to his Chief.

There can be no doubt that Jesus picked him out for one of His inner circle because of his strong attractive traits. He had in him the making of a John, the intimate, the writer of the great fourth Gospel. He might have been a Peter, rugged in his bold leadership of the early Church.

But, though coached and companioned with, loved and wooed, up to the very hour of the cowardly contemptible betrayal, he failed to respond even to such influence as a Jesus could exert. Jesus planned Judas the apostle. He became Judas the apostate, the traitor. He was to be a leader and teacher of the Gospel. He became a miserable reproach and by-word of execration to all men. Jesus' plan failed.

Where the Reproach of Failure Lies.

Will you please mark very keenly that the failure always comes because of man's unwillingness to work with God? It always takes two for God's plan—Himself and a man. All His working is through human partnership. In all His working among men He needs to work *with* men.

Some good earnest people don't like, and won't like, that blunt statement that God fails sometimes. It seems to them to cast a reproach upon God. They may likely think it lacking in due reverence. But if these kind friends will sink the shaft of their thinking just a little deeper down into the mine of truth, they will find that the reproach is somewhere else.

There *is* reproach. Every failure that could have been prevented by honest work and earnest faithfulness spells reproach. And there is reproach here. But it isn't upon God; it is upon man. God's plan depends upon man. It is always man's failure to do his simple part faithfully that causes God's plan to fail.

There is a false reverence that fears to speak plainly of God. It seeks by holding back some things, and speaking of others with very carefully thought-out phrase, to bolster up God's side. True love has two marked traits: it is always plain-spoken in telling all the truth when it should be known; and it is always reverential. It can't be otherwise. The bluntest words on the lips combine with the deepest reverence of spirit. God doesn't need to be defended. The plain truth need never be apologized for.

It's a false reverence that holds back some of the truth, lest stating it may seem to reflect on God's character. Such false reverence is a distinct hindrance. It holds back from us some of the truth, and the strong emphasis that the truth needs to arouse our attention and get into our some-time thick heads. We men need the stirring up of plain truth, told in plainest speech. The Church has suffered for lack of plain telling of the truth. The deepest, tenderest reverence insists upon plain talk, and reveals itself in such talk.

It is irreverent to hold back some of God's truth. For so men get wrong impressions of God. It is unfair as well as irreverent. Theology has sometimes been greatly taken up with adjusting its statements so as to defend God's character. But the plainest, fullest telling of truth is the greatest revealer of His great wisdom and purity and unfailing love.

God's Sovereignty.

There has been a good bit of teaching about "God's sovereignty." Behind that mysterious, indefinite phrase has crept much that badly needs the clear, searching sunlight of day. God's sovereignty is commonly thought of as a sort of dead-weight force by which He compels things to come His way. If a man stand in the way of God's plan so much the worse for the man. It is thought of as a sort of mighty army, marching down the road, in close ranks, with fixed bayonets. If you happen to be on that road better look out very sharply, or you may get crushed under foot.

I do not mean that the theologians put it in that

blunt fashion, nor that I have ever heard any preacher phrase it in that way. I mean that as I have talked with the plain common people, and listened to them, this is the distinct impression that comes continually of what it means to them. Then, too, the phrase has often been used, it is to be feared, as a religious cloak to cover up the shortcomings and shirkings of those who aren't fitting into God's plan.

God *is* a sovereign. The truth of His sovereignty is one of the most gracious of all the truths in this blessed old Book of God. It means that the great gracious purpose and plan of God will finally be victorious. It means that in our personal lives He, with great patience and skill and power, works *through* the tangled network of circumstances and difficulties to answer our prayers, and to bring out the best results for us.

It means further that, with a diplomacy and patience only divine, He works *with* and *through* the intricate meshes of men's wills and contrary purposes to bring out good now—not good out of bad, that is impossible; but good in spite of the bad—and that finally all opposition will be overcome, or will have spent itself out in utter weakness, and so His purposes of love will be fully victorious.

But the practical thing to burn in deep just now is this, that we can hinder God's plan. His plans *have* been hindered, and delayed, and made to fail, because we wouldn't work with Him.

And God *lets* His plan fail. It is a bit of His

The Past Failure

greatness. He will let a plan fail before He will be untrue to man's utter freedom of action. He will let a man wreck his career, that so through the wreckage the man may see his own failure, and gladly turn to God. Many a hill is climbed only through a swamp road.

God cares more for a man than for a plan. The plan is only for the sake of the man. You say, of course. But, you know, many men think more of carrying through the plan on which they have set themselves, regardless of how it may hurt or crush some man in the way. God's plan is for man, and so it is allowed to fail, for the man's sake.

Yet, because the plan is always made for man's sake, it will be carried through, because by and by man will see it to be best. Many a man's character has been made only through the wrecking of his career. If God had had His way He would have saved both life and soul, both the earthly career and the heavenly character.

Let us stop thoughtfully, and remember that God has carefully thought out a plan for every man, for each one of us. It is a plan for the *life*, these human years; not simply for getting us to what we may have thought of as a psalm-singing heaven, when we're worn out down here.

It is the best plan. For God is ambitious for us; more ambitious for you and me than we are for ourselves, though few of us really believe that. But He will carry out His plan—aye, He *can* carry it out only with our hearty consent. He must work *through* our wills. He honors us in that. With greatest reverence be it said that God waits reverently, hat in hand, outside the door of a man's will, until the man inside turns the knob and throws open the door for Him to come in and carry out His plan. We can make God fail by not working with Him. The greatest of all achievements of action is to find and fit into God's plan.

The Church Mission.

Now, God had and has a plan for His Church. That plan is simply this: The Church was to be His messenger to the nations of the earth. There are other matters of vast importance committed to the Church, without doubt: the service of worship and the training and developing of the life of its members. But these, be it said very thoughtfully, are distinctly secondary to the service of taking the Gospel to all men.

These two, the chief and the secondary, are interwoven, each contributing to and dependent upon the other. But there is always a main purpose. And that here, without question, is the carrying of the message of Jesus fully to all the earth. In each generation the chief plan, to which all else was meant to be contributory, was that all men should hear fully and winsomely the great thrilling story of Jesus.

Shall I say that that plan has failed? It hurts too much even to repeat such words. I will not *say* the Church has failed. But I will ask you

The Past Failure

to note God's plan for the Church, and then in your inner heart to make your own honest answer.

And in making it remember the practical point is this—the Church is *you*. *I* am the Church. Its mission is mine. If I say it has failed I am talking about myself. I can keep it from failing so far as part of it is concerned, the part that I am. My concern is not to be asking abstractly, theoretically, about the Church, but about so much of it as I am.

In annual church reports, and triennial and quadrennial, much space is given to telling of the *wealth* of the Church. Of course, I suppose its wealth is meant to be an index of all its work. It may seem a bit odd to use the world's index-finger to point out our faithfulness to our Master's will. It is used, of course, to impress the world in the way the world can most quickly and easily understand.

But the Church was not meant by the Master to be a rich institution in money and property; though it has grown immensely so. The Master's thought was that its power and faithfulness should be revealed entirely in the extent to which all men of all nations know about Himself and have been won to Him.

If we think only a little bit into the past history of the Church, and then into present world conditions, we know the answer to that hurting question about the Church being a failure.

I know that many of you are thinking of the triumphs of the Church; of her imperishable and incalculable influence upon the life of the world. And I will join you heartily in that, some other time. Just now we are not talking of that, but of just one particular fact of its history. One truth at a time makes sharper outlines and brings the whole circle of truth out more plainly.

I love to sing,

> "I love Thy Kingdom, Lord,
> The house of Thine abode;
> The Church our blest Redeemer saved
> With His own precious blood."

We shudder to attempt to think into what these centuries would have been without the influence of the Church.

But at present we are talking about something else. Let me ask you, softly, if God's plan for the Church was that it was to be His messenger to all men, as you think back through nineteen centuries and then think out into the moral world conditions to-day, would you say the plan had succeeded? Or had—?

"*Christ also Waits.*"

There's a bit of light here on that vexed question of the Lord's second coming, about which good, earnest people differ so radically. The Master said, you remember, that we were to be watching for His return. But many ask, how can we be watching when it's been two thousand years since He told us to watch, and the event seems as far off as ever?

I remember one day in a Bible class the lesson

The Past Failure

was in the twelfth of Luke, about watching for the Lord's return. Some of the class seemed to think that it means that we should be in a constant attitude of expectancy, looking for His return. But one man, an earnest, godly old minister said, "How can you be looking expectantly for a *thousand years?*"

But will you mark keenly that the teaching of Jesus Himself was that His return depended on His followers' doing a certain thing?[1] When all men had been told fully of Jesus, then He was to return and carry out a further part of His plan. Clearly if the part we were to play has not been done, it delays His part. The telling of all men about Jesus seems to bear a very close connection with what will occur when Jesus returns.

Some of our good friends have been much taken up with figuring out when the Lord would come back. Some of them seem to have great skill in making calendars. They even go so far as to fix exact dates. They seem to forget that word of the Master, "In such an hour as ye think *not* the Son of Man cometh." If you think He will come at a certain given time, then you can know one thing certainly, that He won't come then.

The only calendar we men have is a calendar of *dates*, fitted to the movements of the sun and moon. God has a calendar, too, but it is a calendar of *events*, not of dates. The completion of His plans doesn't depend on so many revolutions of the earth about the sun, but on the faithful revolution

[1] Matthew 24:14.

of His followers in their movement around the earth telling men of Jesus.

It looks very much as though the Master's coming has been delayed, and His plans delayed, because we have not done the preparatory part assigned us.

"The restless millions wait the light,
Whose coming maketh all things new.
Christ also waits; but men are slow and late.
Have we done what we could? Have I? Have you?"

"*Somebody Forgets.*"

A little fellow, of a very poor family, in the slum section of one of our large cities, was induced to attend a mission Sunday-school. By and by, as a result of the teacher's faithful work, he became a Christian. He seemed quite bright and settled in his new Christian faith and life.

Some one, surely in a thoughtless mood, tried to test or shake his simple faith in God by a question. He was asked, "If God loves you, why doesn't He take better care of you? Why doesn't He tell some one to send you warm shoes and some coal and better food?"

The little fellow thought a moment, and then with big tears starting in his eyes, said, "I guess He does tell somebody, *but somebody forgets*."

Without knowing it, the boy touched the sore point in the Church's history. I wonder if it is the sore point with you or me.

THE COMING VICTORY

Failure Swallowed by Victory.
The Revised Missionary Motto.
Ahead, but Behind.
In a Swift Current.
Power of Leadership.
A Minority Movement.
A Great World-chorus.
The Oratorio of Victory.

The Coming Victory

Failure Swallowed by Victory.

But God's failures are only for a while. They are real. There is the tragic element in them. There is the deep, sad tinge of disappointment running throughout this old Book of God. Yet the failures are only for a time. Sometimes it seems a very long time, especially if you are living through some of it. But the time reaches eagerly to an end. Victory comes. And God's victory will be so great as to make us completely forget the failures that marred the road.

The Eden plan was more than a plan. It was a prophecy of the final outcome. The Book of God begins with failure, but it ends with a glowing picture of great victory, painted with rose colors. Every feature of beauty and of good in Eden has grown greatly in John's Revelation climax. The garden of Genesis becomes a garden-city. All the simplicity and purity of garden life, and all the development and power represented by city life, are brought together. There is now a *river* of *life*, and the *tree* of life has grown into a grove.

And God isn't through with that nation of Israel yet. The Jew can't be lost. In every nation under heaven he can be found to-day, a walking reminder of God's plan. Every Jew, in whatever ghetto he may be found, is an unconscious prophecy of a coming fulfilment of God's purpose. The strange racial immortality of the Jew is a puzzle from every standpoint, except God's. He can't be killed off; though men have never ceased trying to kill him off. The Jew looms up bigger to-day than for many generations.

The present strange restless Jewish longing for national existence again, that will not down, spells out the coming victory of God's plan after centuries of failure. And even though the present tide may run out toward ebb, it will be to gather force for a new and fuller flood. When God's plan works out the world will have a wholly new idea of national life, and of a world-power without army or navy or any show of force, touching all men, and touching them only to bless.

And though King Saul failed, there was already the ruddy David, out among the sheep, waiting the anointing oil, and carrying about in his person his nation's greatest king.

Jesus' Judas failed to realize the promise of his earlier days. He struck the record note for baseness. But Paul was being prepared by blood inheritance and scholarly training. Under the touch of the Master's own hand he became the Church's greatest leader in its life-mission. If Judas struck the lowest note, Paul rang the changes on the highest note of personal loyalty to Jesus and to His world-wide passion and purpose.

The Coming Victory

And the Church has waked up. I said, you remember, last evening, that if you look over the whole history of the Church since its birthday on Pentecost, you are pained by the sore fact that the chief mission entrusted to it has been for the most part forgotten. There has been more forgetting of it, and neglecting it, than fulfilling it.

Yet always, be it keenly noted, in every generation of these centuries there have been those whose vision of Olivet never dimmed. There have always been those who have tried faithfully to carry out the Church's great mission. The darkest days have never been without some of the brightest light, made all the brighter by the surrounding night.

The Revised Missionary Motto.

But there's a new chapter of the Church's life being written as we talk together. Its writing began in the closing twilight of the eighteenth century. That chapter isn't finished yet. Some of its best pages are now being written, with more and better clearly coming.

Its first lines were written by a very common pen. Carey's English cobbler-shop became a sounding-board whose insistent, ringing messages began to waken the Church. The Church is waking up, and shaking itself, and tightening on its clothes, for the greatest work yet to be done in fulfilling the life-mission entrusted to it.

A hundred years ago the fire of God found fresh kindling stuff in the hearts and brains of a few young college fellows in an old New England village. The sore need of the world crowded in upon them by night and by day. But they were few, and young, and unknown. And the task was stupendous. The rain-storm of a Sabbath afternoon drove them to the shelter of a hay-stack. And the storm of the world's need drove them to the shelter of prayer, and then to the shelter of a great purpose. With simple faith in God, and strong devotion to the great neglected task, they spoke out to the Church the thrilling words, "We can do it if we will."

And on that same spot a hundred years later the Church gathered. Those intense words had been heard. The Church had waked up. Men of long service in far-away lands stood with those of the home circle. They talked of the past, but far more of the present and future. They revised the century-old motto. No group of scholars in the Jerusalem Chamber of Westminster Abbey ever did finer revision work. They said, "We can do it, *and* we will." No greater tribute to the memory of the faithful little hay-stack group was ever made than in that changed motto.

The young collegians' bold cry had sounded out throughout the Church. And the Church heard and roused up. The modern missionary movement of the Church is the most marked development of the past century of church history. It can be said that the Church of our day in its missionary activity far exceeds the early Church. That is to say, in certain particulars we have exceeded.

The Coming Victory 139

It is common to refer to the missionary zeal of the first centuries. Fresh from the Master's touch, the early Church was chiefly a missionary church. One great purpose gripped it, and that was to take the news of Jesus everywhere. And they went everywhere. We know most about Paul's journeys in the Grecian and Roman worlds. But there is good evidence that there is another "Acts of Apostles" beside the one bound up in this Bible. Out to the farthest reaches of the earth they seemed to have gone in those early days, preaching and winning men and establishing church societies.

The *bulk* of the modern movement is without doubt greatly in excess of the early movement. The number of men out in various fields, the amount of money being given annually by the Church in America and Great Britain and the Continental countries is so much greater as to leave comparison practically out.

In the thoroughness of organization, the elements of permanency, the great variety of means used such as hospitals, schools, literature, and industrial helps, the present probably exceeds by far the early movement. The statesmanlike study by church leaders of the whole world-field, the steadiness of movement year after year, in spite of difficulties and discouragements, the careful systematic effort to inform and arouse the home church—these are marked features of the present foreign-mission campaign. They are such as to awaken the deepest admiration of any thoughtful onlooker. In all of this the modern Church is making a wholly new record.

Ahead, But Behind.

Yet, while all this is true, it can be said just as truly that the Church, *as a whole*, is so far behind the primitive Church as, again, practically to leave comparison out of the question. *They* were so far ahead in the *mass* of their movement that we are scarcely in the lists at all. Then the *whole* Church was an active missionary society. *Every one* went and preached. The nearest approach to it in modern times probably is the movement of the native Church of Korea. This foreign people seems to have caught the early spirit. Our heathen brothers are taking their place as pace-setters for the Church.

By contrast with that, the modern activity has been by a minority, really a small minority, though a steadily growing one. The leaders have struggled heroically against enormous odds in the backward pull of the majority.

Then they went *everywhere*. That is, they went everywhere that they could, so far as open doors, or doors that could be pried open, let them. We have gone actually farther, and to more places probably, but we haven't begun to go everywhere that we could.

Our ability to go, and the urgent requests for us to come, would carry us to thousands of places not yet touched. If we began to do things as the early Church people did, it would stand out as one of the greatest movements in the history of the race. If a small minority of us have made such enormous strides what could the whole of us do if we would!

In a Swift Current.

The *momentum* of the present missionary movement has been startling. It suggests that we are on the eve of an advance undreamed of by the most enthusiastic. The last twenty-odd years have seen progress clear outstripping that of the previous hundred, though all built upon the foundations so well laid by the earlier leaders of the century.

In answer to the earnest persistent prayer of a few, the Spirit of God found new stuff ready for His kindling fires among the colleges. The story of the prayer of a few that preceded the forming of the Student Volunteer Movement is thrilling. That great movement was literally conceived and brought forth in the travail of prayer. Its widespread influence upon the colleges, and then upon the churches; its early campaigning. its remarkable leaders, its great conventions, the steadiness of its growing influence through more than twenty years, and the distinct mark it has made upon the whole mission propaganda abroad, make up one of the most thrilling chapters of church history, ancient or modern. To-day its influence encircles the earth. Its volunteers are found everywhere.

Its reflex influence upon that other movement,

the Young Men's Christian Association, has been no small part of its work. The two have been interwoven from the beginning, each contributing immeasurably to the other. The practical power of the Young Men's Christian Association on foreign soil is recognized by the Church, and by foreign governments, as of a value clear beyond calculation or statement.

It has come to be one of the great expressions of the unifying spirit of the Church on foreign-mission soil. Our churches at home may go their separate ways, largely. But the pressure of the sore need of the foreign world has been welding the churches there together remarkably. The Christian Associations, both of young men and young women, belonging to all the Church and representing all, have held a strategic position in action, and been of inestimable service to the Church in its missionary propaganda.

The Young People's Missionary Movement, whose long, warm fingers are reaching throughout the whole Church, and the newer Laymen's Missionary Movement with its aggressive campaigning, are both remarkable expressions of the new uprising.

The women of the Church were forehanded in their earnest working and praying. They were up at dawn of day. Their influence is mighty, clear beyond any words to express. And now at last the men are waking up, and the new life is showing itself anew within organic church lines. Men's missionary conventions, with great atten-

The Coming Victory

dances, are swinging into line, and revealing the awakeness of the Church.

Power of Leadership.

The enormous power of personal influence and of devoted leadership has been most marked. In the throng of strong men that lead in all this activity there are two men that by common consent stand out big in the group. Young men they are, both of them, not yet in the full prime of their powers. One has a genius for organization probably never surpassed, if equalled, by military general, or Jesuit chief, or modern captain of industry. The other has mental grasp, keenness of thought, and power of persuasive speech not surpassed by any, if equalled. Both are marked by a singularly deep, tender spirituality, a rare gift of leadership, a poise of judgment, and a devotion to the Church's great mission as true and steady as the polar star.

Around these two young men has grouped up in no small measure this later missionary activity. And it is probably quite within the mark to say that no stronger, abler men can be found in any of the great activities of life to-day in either of these two great English-speaking peoples. It is surely significant that the modern missionary movement rallies around such giants.

It is worthy of special note, too, that the body of men to whom is entrusted the administration of this vast network of foreign service, the foreign-board members and secretaries of the Church, have developed such remarkable power and skill. No body of men has problems more intricate and exacting and difficult. And no body of men in any sphere of activity has shown greater diplomacy and astuteness, hard sound sense, and untiring devotion.

Some good friends are sometimes disposed to be critical of methods and management. They think the affair could be conducted better in some details which they think important. Well, it would be surprising if it were not so. The same criticisms are made of every governmental and great industrial enterprise. Everything human seems to make progress by correcting and improving. But the thing for you and me to keep a critically keen eye upon is this: that no such detail be allowed to affect by so much as a hair's weight the steadfast ardor of our support.

No strong man in the thick of the great driving purpose of his life is turned aside or stopped by the biting or buzzing of a few insects. If even they can't be brushed aside, let them buzz and bite, but don't let the great passion of a life be affected by them. Indeed, they will be clean forgot, even while they are remembered, by the man who has been caught and swept by the fire of his Master's passion for a world.

A Minority Movement.

Yet, be it keenly marked, these great strides have been made by a minority, who have followed the strong leaders. The whole Church is not yet awake. Many protest strenuously against being waked up. The alarm-clocks bother them. Sometimes one is inclined to think that the foreign boards are peculiarly placed between a refrigerator and a furnace.

Missionaries come back home fresh from the front fairly aflame with the fervor of their enthusiasm. Their convictions of what could be done, and should be done, are apt to be spoken out with great positiveness. They seem to some to suggest in an uncomfortable way the thought of a glowing furnace. And many in the home churches seem able to listen with such indifference as to suggest to these returned men and women the chilling air of an ice-box. In between the two sits the Church board engaging in the difficult task of trying to equalize the temperature. But that's merely a detail in passing.

The great fact to mark is that never has the missionary movement bulked so large. And never have such broad statesmanlike plans, such aggressiveness of spirit, coupled with deep devotion, marked the Church in its great life-mission.

One morning at a popular summer resort on the Long Island Sound coast thousands of bathers were enjoying the surf-bathing. The life-saving crew were stationed for duty, on the lookout for any accident. A gentleman standing by one of the crew asked him how he could tell if help were needed. There were thousands of bathers, and a perfect babel of noises. The weather-beaten man, bronzed and toughened and trained to keenness in his work by years of service, said, "I can always hear a cry of distress, no matter how great the noise and confusion. There never yet has been a cry of need I haven't heard."

For a long time the confusion of noises bothered the Church ears. But now the cry of distress from over the wide seas is being heard again distinctly, and is being responded to splendidly. The very earnestness of response and effort is a forerunner of sure victory.

A Great World-chorus.

I recall vividly a scene in Albert Hall in London nearly fifteen years ago. A remarkable gathering from all parts of the world had come together to celebrate the jubilee of the Young Men's Christian Association. About two thousand men had come from the ends of the earth. It was a world-gathering. There were sturdy Englishmen, cosmopolitan Americans, canny Scots, quick-witted Irishmen, sweet-voiced, fervid-spirited Welshmen, and courtly, suave Frenchmen.

Fair-haired, blue-eyed Scandinavians mingled with olive-skinned, black-eyed sons of Italy. The steady-going Hollander and the intense German mingled their deep gutturals with the songs of praise and the discussions. A few turbaned heads, inscrutably quiet almond-eyes, and others of energetic step and speech brought to mind the Great Orient, India and China and Japan. Men won up out of the savagery of Africa sat with Islanders from the Pacific.

The Coming Victory 147

They came from many communions and represented many creeds, and spoke as many tongues as the Jerusalem crowds on the day of Pentecost. But they were drawn together not by their attractive diversity, but because of their oneness. The drawing-power of Jesus was the magnet that drew them. It was the music of His Name that made all their tongues and languages blend and chord in sweet harmony.

This night I speak of they had gathered in the great oval-shaped Albert Hall opposite Hyde Park. With the Londoners, probably, fully ten thousand persons were present. And I think I shall never forget the vast volume of sound, as, led by a chorus of Scandinavian students, they all united in singing, "All hail the power of Jesus' Name."

They didn't sing it to our American tune of "Coronation," but to the old English "Miles Lane." That tune, you remember, repeats over four times the words, "Crown Him," in the last line, gradually increasing in volume, and the fourth time touched with a bit of quieting awe.

I can close my eyes now, and see that great world-gathering and hear again the sweet rhythmic thunder of their singing:

> "And crown Him,
> *Crown Him,*
> CROWN HIM,
> *Crown Him,* Lord of all."

No one can tell to another the thrill and thrall of such a sight and sound. It was all unconsciously a bit of prophecy acted out, faint but distinct, of the great day of victory that is coming.

The Oratorio of Victory.

Have you ever noticed the Oratorio of Revelation? Lovers of music should study the book of the Revelation of Saint John, for its mighty choruses. It is striking just now to notice the double key-note of that closing climactic book of this old Bible. It is this: Satan chained, and Christ crowned. But note for a moment the oratorio sounding its music through these pages.

It opens with a *solo* in the first chapter.[1] John begins writing with steady pen until he seems to get a glimpse of Jesus. Then his pen drops the story, and he begins singing:

> "Unto Him that loveth us,
> And loosed us from our sin by His own blood;
> And hath made us a kingdom,
> Priests unto His God and Father;
> To Him the glory and the dominion
> Forever and ever."

In chapter four[2] comes a *quartette*. The four living creatures round about the throne take up the refrain of John's solo. And, as they sing, their song is caught up by a *sextuple quartette*, twenty-four white-robed, crowned men before the throne.[3]

In chapter five the *Angel Chorus* swings in.[4] They are grouped round about the quartette, and the twenty-four elders. John begins to count

[1] Revelation 1:5, 6.   [3] 4:9–11. 5:8–10.
[2] 4:8.   [4] 5:11–12.

The Coming Victory 149

them. Then his figures give out. His knowledge of mathematics is too limited. There were ten thousand times ten thousand, and unnumbered thousands of thousands. As far as his eye could reach, to left and right, before and behind, was one vast sea of angel faces.

And John listened enraptured and awed, as their wondrous volume of rhythm rang and thundered out. Sweet sopranos and mellow contraltos; ringing tenors and deep basses; first one, then the other, back and forth responding to each other, then all together; marvellous music it must have been.

Then the refrain of their song is caught up by the *Creation Chorus*.[1] Every living creature in heaven and on the earth and under the earth, as though unable to resist the contagious sweep, catch up the music and add their own to it. We don't commonly associate music with the animal creation, nor with nature. It has been said that all the sounds of nature are keyed in the minor, as though some suffering had affected them. We talk of the sighing of the wind, the moaning of the sea-waves, and the mourning of the doves. Though the singing-birds must be excepted. They seem to have caught and kept some of the upper strains.

But evidently something has occurred to strike a new key-note. For now they take up the refrain of the joyous song of the others, and increase the mighty song by their own.

[1] 5:13.

In chapter seven the music has ceased or softened down and is taken up afresh by the *Martyr Chorus*.[1] Again John's figures give out. He declares that nobody could count the multitudes that make up this chorus. It is a polyglot chorus. They sing in many different languages, but all blend into full rhythm. It's a scarred chorus, too. These have been through great tribulation. Their scars tell the mute story of the fierceness of the fight, and the steadiness of their faith.

Through their singing runs a distinct strain of the minor. Its strangely sweet cadence, learned in many an hour of pain, runs as an under-chording through the song of triumph that now fills their hearts and mouths. And as they sing, the angel chorus and the quartette drop to their knees, and swell the wondrous refrain.

In chapter fourteen comes the music of the *Chorus of Pure Ones*.[2] They are gathered close about the person of Jesus. They sing to the accompaniment of a great company of harpers. They sing with a peculiar clearness in their tones. Theirs is a new song. Purity always makes a music of its own, unapproachable for sweetness and clearness.

The *Victors' Chorus* rings out its song in chapter fifteen.[3] These have been in the thickest of the fighting. The smoke of the battle has tanned their faces. They have struggled with the enemy at close range, hip and thigh, nip and

---

[1] 7:9–12.   [2] 14:1–5.   [3] 15:2–4

The Coming Victory 151

tuck, close parry and hard thrust. And they have come off victors. The ring of triumph resounds in their voices, as to the sound of their own harps, harps of God, they add their tribute of song to all the others.

And at the last comes the great *Hallelujah Chorus*, in chapter nineteen.[1] In response to the precentor's call, they all join their voices in one vast melody. The Quartette, the Sextuples, the Angels, the Creation, the Martyrs, the Pure-Ones, the Victors—all sing their song together.

John tries to tell what it was like. His mind went quickly back to earlier days in his home city, Jerusalem, when thousands of pilgrims crowded the temple areas and narrow streets, and spread out over the hills. The unceasing sound of their voices in speech and in their pilgrim songs of praise comes back to him. He says it was like that.

But that isn't satisfactory. It is so much more. He thinks of how the ocean-waves keep pounding, with cannon-roar, on the rocky beach of his Patmos prison isle. So he said it was like that. But still more is needed to give an idea of the vast volume of sound. And he remembers how sometimes the thunders crashed and boomed and roared above him as he lay in his solitude on that lonely bit of sea-girt land. It was like that. It was like all of these together.

And what is it they are singing? Well, there's a variety in the wording of their song, as well as

[1] 19:1–8.

in their voices. But through all runs a refrain that brings back to me the great London chorus. It is this—

> "And crown Him!
> *Crown Him!!*
> Crown Him!!!
> Yes, *Crown Him*
> Lord of all."

It is the rehearsal of the great Oratorio of Victory that we are all to join in singing.

THE CHURCH

Forces that Win.
The Divine Law of Leadership.
God's Messenger.
Reaching out for a World.
"Keep Step."
"Find My World, and Win it Back."

The Church

Forces That Win.

GOD'S world is full of winning forces. The great ball of fire around which our earth revolves is the greatest winning force in the life of the earth. It is constantly winning the earth to itself with a power unseen but tremendous, beyond anybody's power to calculate. The swing of the earth away from the sun is being continually overcome. By an immense drawing power it steadily holds the earth where it can pour down its wealth of warmth and light and life into it.

It woos the moisture up from river and lake and sea, until its gravity partner in the centre of the earth woos it back again in refreshing rain and sheltering snow. It wins out of the earth's warm heart bounteous harvests of grains and fruits, the wealth of forests which affects the earth's life so radically, the flowers with their beauty and fragrance, and the soft carpeting of green to ease the journey for our feet. All the life and beauty of the earth is due to the winning power of the sun.

God Himself is the greatest winning force in all our world. Everywhere men feel the upward drawing toward Him. They may protest against church organizations and creeds, against teachings and long-settled practices and habits of thought, as they do so much, but there is always everywhere a longing in the human heart for God. It is the answer to the longing of His heart for us.

And man is a great winning force. Everywhere men are attracted to each other. There is a winning power within each of us that draws certain others irresistibly to us. And there are winning forces in life that each one of us is powerfully affected by. The old home of earlier days has a marvellous power of attraction for most men. The old fireside, the familiar rooms, the subtle aroma that seems inseparable from the very bricks and boards—who has not felt the tremendous drawing power of these?

What a strange power of attraction a man's mother-tongue has for him. How the heart will give a quick leap, in a foreign land, when, amid a confusing jargon of strange sounds, all unexpectedly some one speaks the dear old familiar words. The person speaking may not be specially congenial or attractive to us, but that sound his tongue gives draws us to him.

The Divine Law of Leadership.

Now I want to talk with you a bit about the forces at hand for winning our old world back to our Father's heart and home. God means us to use all the attractive powers we have in this great world-wooing and world-winning task. The world is to be *won* back, not driven. Men drive men, when they can. But God woos and wins. Man's coming back must be by his own glad, sweet consent. God won't have it any other way.

There are certain strangely winsome forces at our command for winning man. They are mighty in their drawing power. But there are counter-currents that divert and hinder their influence. We need to be familiar with these winning forces, and with the counter-currents, too.

There are seven great forces at our command for this blessed service of soul-winning and world-winning. They are not peculiar to foreign-mission service, for the foreign service itself is not essentially different from other service, except in the greatness of its need. They are the forces for use in all our winning work.

Two of these are distinctly human forces. The first is an organization, the Church. And then that of which the Church is made up, men and women; I mean the power of personality, developed and consecrated personality.

There are two divine forces that work through the human—Jesus and the Holy Spirit. I have put these second in order, because they work through the human. The leadership is in human hands. The initiative of all action is with us. Of course, if you go a bit deeper in, the initiative is with God who moves upon our hearts to make us act. But on the distinctly human level the beginning of service rests in human hands, and these two mighty, almighty, divine forces work through us.

The divine law of leadership and of coöperation in leadership has not always been clearly understood. And there has been bad delay often because of the lack of understanding. Our Lord Jesus in the days of His humanity surrendered Himself to the leadership of the Holy Spirit in His great mission to men. The Spirit worked through Jesus. After Jesus' Ascension the order was reversed. The Spirit yielded Himself to the control of the glorified Son of God. Jesus worked through the Spirit. It was Jesus who sent down the Holy Spirit on the day of Pentecost for the special mission begun that day.

And now, with the greatest awe coming into our hearts at the thought, be it said that these two work through our human leadership. The leadership in service among men is human leadership. The wondrous Spirit of God works through our leadership to reveal Jesus to men in all His winsomeness and power.

There can be no power at all in our human action and leadership except as the Spirit leads and controls us, and is allowed to. And, on the other side, we must not forget, though it has sometimes been forgotten, that God's working waits upon human action and leadership. Memory quickly brings up the fact, so often repeated in the history of the Church, that when men have failed to respond to God's call His work has fallen be-

The Church

hind. Whenever a new chapter of earnest service has been begun it has always been through a new leadership. Some man has listened to God, and let Him have the free use of himself in reaching out to other men.

God needs men. He needs you and me. We are the wire for the transmission of His current of power. The wire is useless without the current. And the current must have the wire along which to travel to its place of service. The divine power is through human action and human leadership. The power is all divine. And the means through which it works is all human. Jesus and the Holy Spirit work through the Church and through each one of us who is willing.

Then there are three spirit forces, or influences, of mighty power in human hands; namely, prayer, and money, and sacrifice.

God's Messenger.

To-night we want to talk about the first of the two human forces—the Church.

We ought to remind ourselves of just what that word "Church" means in this connection. It has many meanings. There are at least two that we should note here in thinking of it as a great winning force. In its broadest meaning, the word is commonly used for the whole group of church organizations taken together, the Roman Catholic and the Greek Orthodox, the Protestant, and the few primitive societies that still retain their old original organization. In the deeper, less used meaning, it stands for the body of those men and women everywhere who are trusting Jesus Christ, and are allied with Him in the purpose of their hearts.

These two meanings, of course, should be the same. All who trust Jesus should be in the church organizations. And all who are in the organizations should be there because of their relation to Jesus. Whatever the facts regarding that may be, the mission of each is the same. And it is with that mission that we are concerned just now.

Jesus planned that His Church should be a great man-winning and world-winning organization. *The* mission of the Church is to take Jesus to all men. It is God's messenger of His truth to all. In that it is the direct lineal descendant and heir of the Hebrew nation.

That nation was chosen to be a messenger or missionary nation. That was the one purpose of its special creation as a nation. It was not to be as the other nations, in the characteristics that commonly mark strong nations. It was to be a *teacher*-nation, receiving its message of truth direct from God, embodying that message in its own life, personally and nationally, and giving it out clearly and fully and winsomely to all the nations of the earth. And, in spite of its failures and breaks, that mission was accomplished to a remarkable extent.

The Church is its heir. It was born in the Jewish nation. It became the heir to its world-

The Church

wide messenger mission. The great commission given by Jesus as He was leaving is the Church's commission for its great life-work. It was spoken to the group of Jewish men who were the nucleus of that body called the Church, that came into being on the day of Pentecost. That ringing, "Go ye into all the world and preach my gospel to the whole creation," is the Master's command to the Church which He brought into being. That is the Church's marching order by which its life is to be controlled and its faithfulness judged.

The scene of the Church's birth gives a vivid picture of its world-mission. It was born in a world-gathering. It was a world-church in its make-up at its birth. Men from all parts of the world became united in one body by the Spirit's touch that great Church birthday. Its birth-gift, the power of speaking many tongues, reveals at once the wide sweep of its service.

It was the Master's plan that His Church should speak all the languages of the earth then and now and always, as well as the language of heaven, the language of love. So every man would learn of Jesus in his native speech. The language of the cradle and of love-making and of the fireside, the language that most quickly kindles the fires in a man's heart, that was the language to be used in carrying Jesus to every man. That was Jesus' plan. The Church was rarely equipped with winning power for a world-service on its birthday in the gift of tongues.

Of course, this is not the only mission of the Church. That is to say, there are other purposes necessarily included in this. Taking the Gospel of Jesus to all men means more than merely taking it and telling it. The teaching and training and developing of those won to Jesus is an inseparable part of the Church mission. The great service of worship has always been recognized as a vital part of the Church life. Sometimes indeed these have been thought of, and still are thought of, as its only mission. But they grow distinctly out of the chief mission and are distinctly contributory and secondary to it. Indeed, they come into being only through the faithful doing of the chief task. Men were won. Then they met for worship and for training.

Reaching Out For a World.

The Church of those first years thoroughly understood what its great mission was to be. The first chapters of the Book of Acts vividly describe the ideal Church as planned by the Master, and as understood by those who felt His own personal touch upon themselves. Everybody went. They went to everybody. They went everywhere. There is pretty clear evidence that they actually went everywhere that men could go. They held their lives, and even their property, subject to the one great gripping purpose.

The greatest leader of the first century of the Church, Paul, who contributed most to its liter-

The Church

ature and exerted the greatest influence upon its life, was above all else a missionary leader. He went practically everywhere. He didn't go hastily, but by carefully thought-out plans. He won men to Christ, organized them into church societies, taught them, and sent them out to win others.

He worked in and out of the world's great city centres of his time. Ephesus, the Asiatic centre, Corinth, the centre of Greek influence, and, Rome, the centre of the world's governing power, were the scenes of his longest and most thorough campaigns. His choice of the centres was a master's strategic choice. For these centres sent their influence out to the ends of the earth. Paul's body might be in Ephesus or Corinth or Rome, but his thought and heart were on the world these cities reached by constant streams of influence.

And to these churches which he had won out of the raw stuff of heathenism he taught the same world-wide message. They became filled with this same world-wide spirit. The Thessalonian and Corinth Churches made their winning power felt throughout Greece and wherever Greek culture had gone, that is to say, everywhere.[1] The Church in Rome sent out the message of Jesus from its golden centre of all Roman roads, out to the farthest reaches of those far-reaching roads.[2]

It is striking, though not surprising, that the days of the Church's missionary activity have been the days of its greatest purity and vigor. When

[1] Thessalonians 1:8. II Corinthians 1:1 l.c. [2] Romans 1:8.

the vision of the Master's face on Olivet, and the ringing sound of His "Go ye" have been lost, the Church has written pages that would gladly be blotted out.

The Church *has* been a winning force beyond any power of calculation or words of description. All that has been done has been done through its activity and leadership. It is to-day a tremendous winning force, reaching its warm hands out to the very ends of the earth, and drawing men to Jesus. With our earnest prayer it will exert a yet mightier influence in taking Jesus to all men and in winning men everywhere to Jesus.

"Keep Step."

The Church is organized Christendom. It stands for the power of organization in God's service. All the vast power of the men and women whose hearts have been renewed by the Holy Spirit can be brought to bear at a given point with tremendous force through the Church. That was and is the Master's plan.

Organization is rhythmic action, a crowd of men working by agreement as one man. Never was the world so impressed with the almost magical power of organization as to-day. Never has organization been brought up to so high a pitch of efficiency. The unparalleled progress of the world in our day is due to the marvellous skill that has been developed in organized action.

Now, this almost omnipotent power of organization was meant to be used in winning the world

The Church

back home. That is the meaning of the birth of the Church on that great Pentecost day. It is remarkable that the most perfectly matured bit of organization, in this day of matured and perfected organizations, is a church. For by common consent of thoughtful students the most finely adjusted and thoroughly matured bit of human machinery is the Roman Catholic Church.

If such a masterpiece of organization were controlled by the Spirit that controls in these early chapters of Acts, what tremendous and thorough and rapid work would be done in world-winning! And that is the goal toward which we should be driving. The evangelization of the whole world is *an easy task* for the whole Church. It would be a stupendous, if not an impossible task for the few. It has been a gigantic task for the leaders, who by dint of great planning and persuasion and earnest pleading have done as much as has been done. But if the whole Church or half of it were to go at it as earnestly as men go at other things, it would be an easy task.

I remember one October morning walking across an old smoke-begrimed bridge that spans the Ohio at Cincinnati. My eye was caught by a dingy sign in large plain letters nailed up in a prominent place. It simply said, "Processions in crossing this bridge must break step." That was all. But it was imperative. It was a law. The processions *must* break step. The same men might cross the bridge, in as large numbers, at the same time, but they must not keep step.

The authorities knew perfectly well that for a body of men to march *in step*, every left foot set down at once, the impact of every right foot striking at the same moment, would so—I do not say, *add* to the force exerted—would so *multiply* the force exerted upon the bridge as to endanger its safety. The power of concerted action is immense beyond any power of conception. Every bit of power at command can so be brought to bear at one point with a force beyond any words to express.

Our Master reverses for us the old bridge sign. Out from Pentecost rings this word: "Let my followers all form in line, close ranks, and move out to a world conquest, and—*keep step*." That command of His will make a winning force so great as to shorten up the world's present calendars, and shorten up the world's pain, and lengthen out the new life that will come to untold numbers through Jesus.

"Find My World and Win it Back."

Nearly forty years ago David Livingstone, one of the Church's great world-winning pioneers, was lost in the depths of equatorial Africa. That is to say, he had advanced so far ahead of everybody else that the rest of us lost track of him, and so we called him lost. Perhaps we got the use of the word twisted, and we were the lost ones because we hadn't kept up. He had gone where the Church was told to go, but the rest of us had lingered behind, and so the main column be-

The Church 167

came detached from its leader. Everybody was talking about the lost leader.

James Gordon Bennett, the owner of the *New York Herald*, sent a telegram to one of its correspondents, Henry M. Stanley. Bennett was in Paris, and Stanley at Gibraltar. The telegram summoned Stanley to come to Paris at once. Stanley went, reached Paris at midnight, knocked at the great newspaper-man's door, and asked what was wanted. "Find Livingstone," was the short, blunt reply. "How much money do you place at my disposal?" asked Stanley. "Fifty thousand dollars, or a larger sum. Never mind about the money; find Livingstone."

Stanley went. It took two years' time to get ready. It required a specially planned campaign and thorough preparation. The planning was done, and the world was thrilled when the bold missionary leader was found.

Our Master has sent a message to His Church. It is written down in a Book, and is being repeated by wireless messages constantly. He says, "Find my world, and bring it back; never mind about the expense of money and lives. *Find my world and win it back.*" And the Church has the winning power to do it.

EACH ONE OF US

OUR DRAWING POWER.
SOWING OURSELVES IN LIFE'S SOIL.
OUR NEED OF A WORLD TO WIN.
LIVING BROAD LIVES IN NARROW ALLEYS.
GIVING GOD FREE USE OF OURSELVES.
GROWING BIGGER FOR SERVICE'S SAKE.
MY MISSION-FIELD.
OUR SPIRIT-TOUCH.

Each One of Us

Our Drawing Power.

THE greatest human winning force is a man swayed in every bit of his being by the Spirit of Jesus. Man himself is the most attractive thing on God's earth. He has the greatest drawing power.

He is attractive to God. He drew out of the creative power of God this world of beauty and splendor. He drew Jesus down from the throne of God to the earth, to poverty and hard labor, to the limitations of human life, to misunderstandings and suffering and pain and death. These were gladly yielded to because it was all for man. How the crowds used to draw Jesus! He would give His strength out to them without stint, until those closest to Him, not understanding, sought to interfere for the sake of his strength.

One man was a sufficient magnet to draw him away from His rest, and to draw out of Him the best of love and strength He had. Nicodemus' earnest presence wooed out of His busy life a whole evening, and drew out the matchless words that the world has been feeding upon ever since. The woman of little half-breed Sychar, though an outcast, drew from Him the touch of power that transformed her life and her village.

Man is attractive to his fellows. There is no power so attractive to a man as another man. The phenomenal growth of modern cities is one of the evidences of this. Everywhere men acknowledge the attractiveness that their fellows have for them. Every friendship, every leadership, every family circle, and gathering of men for whatever purpose tells of the winning power that man has for his fellows. It is modified by all sorts of surrounding conditions, and exists in many different degrees. The great leader and the great orator have it in unusual measure. Every man has some of it. Each man is a magnetic north pole. Every man of his spirit-current is drawn toward him with a steady pull.

Man can win man. That fact at once brings out strikingly his winning power. For the hardest thing in all this world to win is a man. Of all luggage man is the hardest to move. He won't move unless he will move. Only as the string is tied inside to his will can he be persuaded to move. The heart may help open the door into the will. Most often that is the way to get in. Sometimes intelligence, the reasoning powers, open the way in, but rarely; often these two, the heart and the reason, combined. But even then they go tandem, with the heart in the lead; only man can get that door open, and tie the tether to the other man's will, and draw him out, whither he will. He can do it. And only he can. Man yields to the drawing power of his fellow.

With the deepest reverence be it said that when God would redeem a world He sent a Man. Aye, He came as a man. And, while Jesus was so much more than man, we must always insistently remind ourselves that He was truly and fully a man. He was as really human in every bit of His make-up and life as though only human. Because of man's power to win his fellow, Jesus came to the man-level, as a Man, that so He might win men.

Sowing Ourselves in Life's Soil.

Man is winsome, wherever found, just as he is. He may be shackled and slimed over with sin, as he plainly is. He may have lost much of his winsomeness, as probably he has, through deeply rooted prejudice and superstitions, and endless limitations of surroundings and education, but he still remains a powerful magnet to his fellow.

But he is most winning in his winningness as he returns to the original as God planned him. His native winning power comes out fully only as sin is taken out of him, washed out, and burned out; the desire for it removed, and the hurt of sin upon his bodily and mental powers overcome. Jesus is the sort of human that God planned. And only as He is allowed to come into a man's life, and treat the sin trouble at the core, and rule from within, can man come to his own in his rare winsomeness.

Only *won* men can win men, of course. Only the man who has felt the power of Jesus can tell some one else of that marvellous power. Nobody else wants to. Nobody else can. For nobody else knows that power. But that man must. There is something inside that compels him to. The man who realizes most keenly that he has been saved will be the most intent on getting others saved, too. The passion for Jesus becomes a passion for telling others about Jesus.

Jerry McCauley must spend out his life in Water Street because he had been gripped by the Man who spent out His life for him. The passion is irresistible. Splendid young Hugh Beaver must win the Pennsylvania students to Jesus because Jesus had become the magnet of his own life. Livingstone must plunge into the depths of the African wilds, and Duff into India's heat, and Hudson Taylor into China's inner provinces because of the Jesus-passion that gripped them.

Now the thing to mark very keenly is this: that God's chief reliance in His passionate outreach for His world is *men*. He is counting on you and me. The power that actually wins men is the power of God. Only He can so play upon human wills and hearts as to induce them gladly to open to Him. That is true. But it is as true that only *through* the winsome power of men can He use His winning power fully.

I am not going to take up just now why this is so, though that is full of helpful suggestion. But simply to have you mark that straight through this old Book, and through church history, and in actual experience this has been His way of reaching men. God's pathway to one human heart is through another human heart.

When men have failed Him God's plan has failed. His sovereignty doesn't mean that His plan doesn't fail. It means here that with endless patience He clings to the failed plan until He can get the man through whom it can be carried out. But meanwhile there has been serious delay and sad suffering for man.

There is a most striking sentence spoken by Jesus in explaining the parable of the tares, in Matthew, Chapter thirteen. He said, "The good seed are the sons of the kingdom." We think of the truth, the Gospel message, as the good seed that we are to sow, and so it is. But there's a far better seed. It is men, saved men. We are to sow our saved selves, our lives, in the soil of men's lives. Our presence among men was meant to be God's greatest sowing of the seed of life. Upon that seed He sends the dew and rain and sunlight of His Spirit. And through that sort of sowing He wins His greatest harvests.

Our Need of a World to Win.

Now I want to turn aside here a bit, and say this: we men need a world to win. The world needs winning. There's no doubt of that. And just as really we men need a world to win. We need the impetus and stimulus, the grip and the swing of having a world to win. The Master's command fits with great exactness into the need of our lives.

Every man needs a great purpose to grip his

life. So he is anchored and held steady against the world's tidal movements. If he isn't tied to some great gripping purpose the wash of the sea will send him adrift, or the fierce undertow will suck him under. And many are adrift. And many are in the deadly suction of the undertow.

Jesus' command provides the great purpose that every man needs to hold him steady and to bring out, and bring out best, all the splendid powers with which we are endowed. When we are not gripped by the great purpose planned for us we swing off into smaller, meaner purposes.

I mean, of course, those of us who are awake. Many people are habitual somnambulists. All their walking and moving about is done in a state of sleep. Some men never wake up. They go through the motions of life so far as they must. The mechanism of habit keeps certain motions going, but the real man within is asleep or dozing, with occasional spells of being sleepily awake.

But men who are awake, and doing something, find a vent for their energy on some lower level. The God-given energy will move out and stir itself to action. But, having somehow missed the real purpose planned for them, they allow the lower purposes to grip them. They organize great affairs, or less great, industrial, intellectual, political, fraternal, social, and spend their energy on these. It is the response they make to the call of their natures for some great gripping purpose. But it looks very much like another case of meeting a request for bread with cold hard stones.

Each One of Us

These things in themselves are right, of course; so far as they are right. They belong in the scheme of life. They should be given full place in one's life. But that place is always a distinctly secondary place. They belong in as number two.

A Christian business man gives most of the day and year to his business, and gives of the best of his thought and strength to it. But if he have gotten his bearings straight, his business is not in first place. It is made to serve something higher. It earns the gold with which to finance the great purpose of Jesus' life, and of his own life, namely, the purpose of winning men, and of winning a whole world of them. How it would sweeten business and fraternal and social contacts and friendships, if the salt of this great purpose seasoned them!

Living Broad Lives in Narrow Alleys.

We need the *bigness* of this great purpose. So many lives are dwarfed by their very littlenesses. We are bothered with being short-sighted. The eyeglasses of the Master's purpose for us would wondrously widen out our scope of vision. And through the new eyes would come broader, farther, clearer views, and changed action. The littleness of our ideas would be amusing if it were not so distressing.

I recall one day riding on a Fort-Wayne train through Indiana. I chanced to overhear a bit of conversation. Two men, chance acquaintances, were talking. One of them had his home in Elkhart. The other asked him where Elkhart is. By the side of the Elkhart man there sat a little sweet-faced boy. Instantly, as the question was asked, he looked up with surprised eyes, and said, "Don't you know where Elkhart is? Why, Elkhart is down where I live."

The amusing childish words seemed to have a familiar sound. I seem to have run across a few people whose idea of God's world is about on the level of the small boy's. The world is where they live. The rest is a hazy, vague something, or—nothing. It exists for them, if it exists at all in their thoughts.

"Living for self, for self alone, for self and none beside;
    Just as if Jesus had never lived, as if Jesus had never died."

It would be pitiable and pathetic enough if only these people themselves were concerned in their poor, stunted, narrow-alley living. But it is more than that; it is tragic, because of the multitude of brothers, here and abroad, sorely needing the help that was meant to go out to them through us.

Then most men live narrow lives so far as the daily round is concerned. The home, or shop, or store, or office is their daily horizon, with practically the same round of duties day after day, year in and year out. The very narrowness of the round tends to make narrow people. They get into as much of a rut in their thinking as their daily action is apt to become. Their work runs in fixed grooves that are apt to become fixed ruts. And this makes ruts in their thinking. Their souls seem to grow small by the very smallness and sameness of the daily tread. That is the life of the great crowd of men all over the world.

It's an immense relief to see something big. Big things always attract. Is it partly because our daily round is so narrow and small? Jesus plans a bigness that shall refresh us constantly. We have hearts big enough to hold a world, and brains able to plan for a planet, even while our feet tread the same old shut-in path.

A young man may be going a commonplace, treadmill sort of grind, in a small corner of some great manufacturing concern, and be at the same time carrying on a bigger enterprise than the president of his concern. For he may be planning and praying for a world, and actually lifting it up in the arms of his strong purpose toward the level of God.

The shipping clerk may be hammering in barrel-heads all day long, but each blow may help emphasize the prayer of his heart for China, or India, or his Sunday-school class.

"Forenoon, afternoon, and night,
Forenoon, afternoon, and night,
Forenoon, afternoon, and what? no more?
The empty song repeats itself. Yea, that is life.
Make this forenoon sublime, this afternoon a psalm,
This night a prayer, and time is conquered, and thy
   crown is won."

The Master's gracious plan is that we shall have the refreshment of doing big things. We are made for big things. They help us grow into the big size that belongs to us. World-winning is a great boon to the crowd compelled by the habit of life to tread a narrow path.

Giving God Free Use of Ourselves.

Now the great question every earnest man asks himself is, How can I be of most use to God and my fellows? I want to suggest three things that have helped me in answering that question. It may be that they will help you, too, in getting your answer to it.

First of all is this: that we let God have the free use of us. Whatever I am, whatever gifts and opportunities I have—these I will turn over to God, that He may have the fullest and freest use of them. God asks from each of us *a consecrated personality*. And "consecrated" simply means that I give God the use of myself, and that He makes use of what I have given to Him. That's the double meaning of the word in the Bible.

My personality, that is, what I am in myself, is the chief thing I have in life. It is through this personality, which men recognize as I, that the Spirit of God works in His reaching out for others. My personality is the make-up of all that I am. My presence is that subtle something that combines all that I am. It clings to me wherever I go. Men know it by my name. Out through it goes the power of the man within.

The body, the glance of the eye, the quality and intonation of the voice, the way the body is carried,

Each One of Us 181

and the something more than these that unites them into one—these go to make up the presence, the outer shell of the personality. All the power within makes itself felt through this. A man's mere presence is an immeasurable influence.

There is a subtle, intangible, but very real spirit influence breathing out of every man's presence. It is proportioned entirely to the strength of the man living within. With some it is very attractive. Sometimes it is positively repulsive. It is the expression of the man within. The presence becomes the mould of the spirit within, large or small, noble or mean, coarse or fine, as he makes it. The strength of a man's will or its weakness; the purity of his heart or its lack of purity; the ideals of his life, high or low; the keenness or slowness of his thinking—all these express themselves in his presence.

We know the difference between a man of strong presence and one whose presence is weak; though very few of us are skilled in reading, except in a very small way, the character it reveals; through our presence each of us is constantly influencing those with whom we come in contact. Now this is the chief thing we have for our winning work. This is the thing that Jesus uses. It is this that the Spirit of God takes possession of, if He may, and that He uses in His outreach to others. We win most and best through what we are.

Now, of course, I do not mean that we are to be thinking of it that way all the time. The thinking that you have a winsome presence would itself rob you of the most winsome part of it. Winsomeness of presence is greatest and sweetest when we are wholly unconscious that there is such a thing about us. As we are absorbed in Jesus, and in our fellows, the winsomeness that is native to us shines out most attractively. It has been covered up and hidden away a good bit by sin. Some men seem to have none. Some have a great deal, in spite of their ignoring of God.

But as He is allowed to play upon us, as we seek to let His Spirit rule our conduct and control our powers, the original God-image comes out. This is a return to natural conditions as planned by God. What has been lost through sin is restored and grown bigger and richer by the Spirit's presence. I can give God the full use of this precious gift of personality.

Growing Bigger for Service's Sake.

There's a second thing to do. This consecrated personality can be made *a developed personality*. We don't start into life full size. We have to grow. The greatest task of life, as well as one of the sweetest, is in growing fine in grain, and big in size, and skilled in action. The highest achievement of life and the rarest to find is self-mastery, that is, all that one is in himself grown big and fine-grained, skilfully used and held steadily to its true use. All other achievements are through this one.

The stronger I can make my body the more I can give God to use. The more thoroughly I can understand the great, simple laws of my body, and the more I can get into the habit of obeying them, the more can God use me in His plans. Such common things as eating and drinking, breathing and exercising, sleeping and resting and dress, may not be called common any more, if through thoughtfulness here you and I can be of greater use to our Master and our fellows.

The keener and clearer and stronger we can make our thinking, by dint of self-discipline, the greater power have we with other men. The purer the heart, the loftier the practical ideals that control the personal habits, the greater is the winning power at command.

We may not be conscious of the difference. We will not be thinking of that. But the increased power of attraction is there, and is breathing out of one's presence, and is distinctly felt by others. And, more, it is making a distinct mark upon others, more than they know. We must set ourselves to growing bigger and better for service's sake.

My Mission-field.

The third thing is *a world-wide vision*. That is to say, our thinking and planning and praying and giving shall be on a world scale. There is nothing remarkable about this. The strangely remarkable thing is that there is so little of it. Man was made on the world size. It is natural to us to grasp the world in our thinking and action. This other thing of living on a smaller scale is the cramping effect of sin. We were made big. We are big. We need a big world. We enjoy bigness. We get this from God. We are truest to ourselves as we live on the world plan. The world was given us originally to subdue, and now to win.

This does not mean to neglect anything or anybody nearby. It's a bit of the cramping of sin that anybody thinks so. The man who spreads a map of the world beside his open Bible in the morning or evening prayer-hour is likely to have a warm hand for the fellow next him. We are made that way, to grasp the globe, *and* each thing close at hand that needs our care. That's a bit of the image of God in us. As we allow Him sway, the original power is restored to us.

One result of this will be that many of us will go in person to some far-away part of the great world-field. That's a serious thing to do, requiring some special qualification of body and of training. For the task out there is a great one. There are trying conditions to be met. The very best is called for.

If a man may go in person to the foreign field he is greatly favored. Let nothing hold him back. It is a privilege to serve anywhere. But the highest privilege of service is out there. Many cannot go; and many may not go. Some are plainly bidden to stay. The home administration

Each One of Us

of the missionary enterprise requires strong men at home.

A second result will be that wherever we are, will be a mission-field to us. We are, where we are, *to give,* not to get. Whether in far-off China or maybe in some disillusioned commonplace home town, we will be winning men to Jesus all the time *by direct touch.* The mastering thought will be to let the wondrous Spirit reach out through us, freely and fully, unhindered by anything in us, and so touch every one whom we touch.

In any circle, business or social, our hearts will be saying, "I am among you as he that serveth." Consciously, by direct word, by indirect touch, with love's rare diplomacy we will win men. Unconsciously, by our presence, we will as really be winning them.

No one has an imagination vivid enough, or words graphic enough, to tell the power of that direct human touch. All life is athrill with its magic. Even when it becomes less direct, a bit removed from the personal, its power is indescribably great.

John Eliot's work among the Massachusetts Indians kindled David Brainerd. Brainerd's flame touched Jonathan Edwards. Edwards' pamphlet on "Extraordinary Prayer for a Revival of Religion and the Advancement of Christ's Kingdom on Earth" suggested to William Carey the plan of an organized society. Fire spreads. Where the touch of God comes the fire of God goes out through that human touch.

Our Spirit-touch.

A third result will be this: we will be reaching out and winning men in all the rest of the world by *our spirit-touch*. You may be in some African fastness or in the midst of China's age-old civilization or just here at home, but you can be exerting a tremendous spirit-power that can be felt out to the ends of the earth.

It will all be in the Name of Jesus. It will be in the power of the Holy Spirit. Only in that Name and through the Spirit can such winning influence be exerted at all. So a man can have spirit-touch with the man by his side. And just as truly he can have spirit-touch with men at the farthest reach of the earth.

There is a spirit influence going out from each of us in addition to that which goes through the direct personal touch. It is not a conscious influence. That is, we are not concsious that it is being exerted. It goes out from us as we pray. It goes out of us as our thought is centered on those far-away parts and peoples. Its strength will depend on the strength of one's personality.

We are familiar with the fact that a man of strong personality has a greater influence upon his fellows whom he touches directly than a weaker man has. It is just the same with regard to one's spirit-touch. The stronger and keener and purer I may become, the more I know of the self-mastery which comes through Jesus-mastery, the

Each One of Us

greater force can I exert as a winner of men, both by direct touch and by spirit-touch.

Will you kindly come up nearer in spirit, as we close our talk together, and let me ask softly: Have we given the free use of ourselves to the Master? Are we growing ourselves into bigger-sized, finer-grained, better-controlled men and women daily? For the Master is depending on us. He is counting much on having the use of us. He can reach out to the very ends of the earth through *each one of us*. May we not fail Jesus!

JESUS

Jesus Draws Men.

Jesus Draws out the Best.

Many Doors, but One Purpose.

Make it a Story.

How Peter Told Paul.

"A More Excellent Way."

Jesus

Jesus Draws Men.

THE great heart-magnet is God. No one is so winsomely attractive as He. His winning power is beyond any other. Man is winsome. But it is because God made him winsome, and re-makes him yet more winsome. He gave him a bit of His own self. That's the secret of all our human winsomeness.

Now Jesus is God to us. We know God only as we know Jesus. Jesus is the heart of God beating in time and tune with human hearts. Nobody is so winsome as Jesus. All the native winsomeness of man and all the divine winsomeness of God combine and blend in Him. He has always drawn men to Himself. And He still does, and always will.

He drew men of all classes when He was down here. The reverent star-students of far-away Babylon were drawn to His birth by a compelling they could not resist. He drew the thoughtful, scholarly men of His own nation, such as Nicodemus of the inner, highest circle. And He drew military officials of high rank and wealth in the service of imperial Rome. By the same power the half-breed, despised Samaritans and the earnest seekers after truth from cultured Greece were drawn to Him.

The plain farmer people of Galilee, and the hardy fisherfolk, and hard-handed laboring-men came as eagerly to him. He drew the pure, fine-grained, gentle Mary of Bethany, with her unusual keenness of spirit insight; and drew as well the unnamed outcast woman, steeped in sin, who was forgiven much, and who loved much, and so gave much.

Practical hard-headed men of sharp bargains and shrewd trading, like Matthew, felt His pull upon their hearts equally with men of pure heart and lofty ideals like Nathanael. By special effort, for a special purpose He drew high-bred, high-strung, scholarly, intense Paul, out of his mad enmity into a lifelong devotion.

The crowds came until His daily routine and ministering help were repeatedly and seriously interrupted. And strong men sought Him alone to lay bare the longings and questionings of their hearts. His Roman judge felt the strange winsomeness of His presence and speech, though lacking in the courage to follow his convictions regarding Him. And the Roman officer in charge of His execution was forced to admit the power of His presence.

All the world gathered about His cross. Representatives from all parts, in large numbers, were at the Jerusalem feast; and on that morning, by common consent, they were drawn out to the place where He hung.

He even drew the arch-tempter. He came with his subtlest temptations, and bitterest enmity, and most malignant cunning. Could there be greater evidence, by contrast, of the drawing power of His purity and goodness and steadfast devotion to His mission?

Jesus Draws Out the Best.

And Jesus had the power to draw out of men the best there was in them. Possibilities, traits, and powers that neither they nor their friends supposed they had came out into strong life under the spell of His touch. There seemed to be something in Him that drew the same sort of thing out of them.

Out of Simon, the hot-headed, impulsive fisherman, He drew the steady man of rock. Out of fiery John, the son of thunder, He drew the man of tender, strong love. And out of quiet, retiring Andrew He drew a man with a reputation for bringing others to Jesus.

He drew out of the Sychar outcast a sense of her sin, and then a winner of souls; and out of that other woman of open sin, a longing for purity that paved the way to all else that came. Under His compelling touch there came out of the blind-born man a willingness to sacrifice all for such a Master; and out of James, the other son of thunder, a courage to endure suffering that men had not known he had.

That was when He was down here, a man. And ever since that fleecy cloud received Him out of sight He has been drawing men of all the world. And time would as utterly fail me, as it did the writer of the Hebrews, if I tried to tell of the men He has drawn. Men of every rank, high and low, in every nation, savage and civilized, in every generation of all these centuries have felt the thrill of His power. And they have followed Him at the cost of all that men hold most dear.

And He is just the same to-day. He is as available now in all His drawing power wherever men meet, in city slum and savage wild, in college hall and business street, among the philosophical and cultured, and among the ignorant and untrained. If we will take Him to them, and let Him out through our lips and lives, He will draw men up the heights. He can draw against any power of downward suction, and He will. He promised to draw men, if lifted up. And He has never failed to do it.

Now, it is this drawing Jesus that men need and want. There is an enormous advantage in taking Jesus to men, because there is a something inside men everywhere that responds to Jesus. That something may be choked and covered up, crowded down and fought against, as it is. But it is there. When you take Jesus to a man you may know that you are taking a supply to a demand. You are bringing a man the answer to his heart's questions. It is as the coming together of two parts that belong together, but have been held apart by some hindrance.

That hindrance is stubborn. It has to be

Jesus

fought. It can be overcome. That's the chief task. Then the part in man that answers to Jesus eagerly fits into its place in Him. That coming together is always blessed, beyond words. Everywhere men of all sorts and ranks and degrees of savagery and culture eagerly respond to Him. And they declare that they find in Him the full answer to their deepest longings.

Many Doors, but One Purpose.

It is this marvellous magnet, Jesus, that we are to take to men; not theology, nor education, nor medical skill, nor hospitals, nor industrial helps, except incidentally. These are the tin cup which one is glad to use to give the thirsty traveller water from the spring.

You will understand at once that I have no thought of criticizing theology or of discrediting it, if I could. It has its place. But that place is not out in the thick of the crowd, but back in the quiet hall of study. There must be thorough study and systematic putting together of the truth. There needs to be patient plodding and mental drilling.

You have no need to be told of the immeasurable value of the splendid foundation building of Christian scholars. But this is school work, in the main. It is to make us better workmen. So a man gets his bearings and poise. But the people down in the dust and drive of the crowd don't want theology. They want Jesus. It is striking that everywhere men want to hear about Jesus.

Educational work has played an indispensably great part in the scheme of missions. But the purpose of it, of course, is to make an open door for the entrance of Jesus into men's lives. It is invaluable in itself alone, regardless of any other purpose. But the teacher of any sort of learning in the mission school, who is chiefly absorbed in the teaching itself instead of using it as a means to something higher, is missing the whole purpose of his work.

And what words can be used strong enough in speaking of the blessed work of medical men in foreign-mission lands? These skilled, patient, faithful men and women in hospital and dispensary and private service are doing a work of incalculable value. It should be done even if the bodily results were all. But the underlying purpose through it all is to lead men to know Jesus. And no one has such a short, quick road into a man's heart as he who can relieve his body.

These things are doorways into men's lives; and great doorways, too. They are well worth all the money and lives expended if they went no farther than body and mind and better conditions. But the main purpose in them is to find a way into men's hearts, and take in Jesus; that so men may get the greater as well as the less.

Make it a Story.

Now, how shall we best tell men of Jesus? Well, the modern newspaperman's rule in his work is this: "Make it a story." This is his lead-

Jesus 197

ing rule in all his writing work. Whatever the occasion may be, whether a meeting of scholars or an accident on the street, it is to be put into story-form. That is the ideal toward which he works. All the descriptions, and quotations, and information, and philosophizings are to be woven into this web. They know that a story is the easiest thing to read and to listen to, and also the hardest to tell well.

That should be our rule here: *Make it a story about Jesus.* When it comes to talking the Gospel to a group of people, large or small, in New York or Shanghai, make it a story. Wherever you may begin the story, see that its purpose is to lead up to Jesus. You may use twenty-five minutes in getting your story out, and then put the Jesus touch in the last five minutes. But as they go away that last five has given its flavor to the whole half-hour's talk. Or, you may begin with Him, and so run through. But the rule should be: Make it a simple, natural, attractive story, such as people will want to listen to, because it interests them.

That means a lot of hard work in preparation. The simpler and easier and more natural it seems to the crowd the more it will have cost you in study. You will have to study so carefully that they won't guess you have studied at all. You must absorb this Bible story, bit by bit, through and through, until it becomes a bit of yourself.

You must use books that help make this Book clearer and plainer. That is really the mission of biblical books, to make *the* Book plainer. If they send you to the Bible they have fulfilled their mission. If you stay in them, they have failed.

The Bible is an Oriental book in its way of putting things. Its story is built upon the habits of those Eastern peoples. While it is full of simple teaching easily understood, one needs to understand those habits to get the real meat of the meaning. This means a habit of hard work for him who would be a winner of men. He should have an ambition to know the Bible story thoroughly, and to get it from the Bible itself.

But, whatever your particular message may be at any time, let it lead up by a straight road to Jesus. Follow the rule of the Book itself here. The Old Testament all points to Jesus. It can be understood only as He is understood. And the New is aflame with His presence. Tell the story of Jesus to men. They never tire of that. Tell it accurately. Tell it simply. Tell it with endless variety. Put it in simple every-day words, so they think about the story and not about you or your words.

Tell Jesus' life; His characteristics; how He mingled among men, and talked with them. Take up the Gospel incidents, and give them their natural flavoring and coloring in present-day speech. Tell of the Nazareth life, in home and carpenter shop and village. Go through those wondrous three and a half years, bit by bit.

Go into the temptation wilderness, out on the blue waters of Galilee, and into Gethsemane's olive-grove. Climb that bit of a rise of ground called Calvary. Wherever you are in that story, make sure that the coloring of Calvary gets distinctly in, by word or phrase or climax or somehow.

Now, of course, there will be some theology in your telling. You will make comments and explanations. And preachers call that theology. That is unavoidable. That is the place for such teaching, as it naturally grows out of the story. But the story should be the main thing. Men should be sent away thinking about a Man, Jesus; not about a theory of doctrine.

How Peter Told Paul.

I remember very distinctly one time Mr. Moody was speaking at the Ohio Sunday-school Convention in Cleveland. He was saying that teachers should open up the Bible and make it attractive. Then he told the story of how, in '84, in London he was talking with a lawyer friend who had just come down from Edinburgh. He had been hearing Andrew Bonar preach up there, and was greatly taken with his way of preaching.

Mr. Moody told the story something like this:

"Bonar was preaching in Galatians, where it says that Paul went to Jerusalem to see Peter, and he said that he could imagine Peter saying to Paul, 'Would you like to take a walk?' and Paul said he would, so they went down through the streets of Jerusalem, over the brook Kidron, arm in arm, and Peter stopped and said, 'Look,

Paul, this is the very spot where He wrestled and where He suffered, and sweat great drops of blood. There is the very spot where John and James fell asleep, right there. And right here is the very spot where I fell asleep. I don't think I should have denied Him if I hadn't gone to sleep, but I was overcome. I remember the last thing I heard Him say before I fell asleep was, "Father, let this cup pass from me if it is Thy will." And when I awoke an angel stood right there where you are standing, talking to Him, and I saw great drops of blood come from His pores and trickle down His cheeks. It wasn't long before Judas came to betray Him. And I heard Him say to Judas, so kindly, "Betrayest thou the Master with a kiss?" And then they bound Him and led Him away. And that night when He was on trial I denied Him.'

"He pictured the whole scene. And the next day Peter turned again to Paul and said, 'Wouldn't you like to take another walk to-day?' and Paul said he would. That day they went to Calvary. And when they got on the hill Peter said, 'Here, Paul, this is the very spot where He died for you and me. See that hole right there? That is where His cross stood. The believing thief hung there, and the unbelieving thief there on the other side. Mary Magdalene and Mary, His mother, stood there, and I stood away on the outskirts of the crowd.

" 'The night before, when I denied Him, He looked at me so lovingly that it broke my heart, and I couldn't bear to get near enough to see Him. That was the darkest hour of my life. I was in hopes that God would intercede and take Him from the cross. I kept listening, and I thought I would hear His voice.' And he pictured the whole scene, how they drove the spear into His side, and put the crown of thorns on His brow, and all that took place.

"And the next day Peter turned to Paul again and asked him if he wouldn't take another walk. And Paul said he would. Again they passed down the streets of Jerusalem, over the brook Kidron, over Mount Olivet, up to Bethphage, and over to the slope near Bethany. All at once Peter stopped and said: 'Here, Paul, this is the last place where I ever saw Him. I never heard Him speak so sweetly as He did that day.

"'It was right here He delivered His last message to us, and all at once I noticed that His feet didn't touch the ground. He arose and went up. All at once there came a cloud and received Him out of sight. I stood right here gazing up into the heavens, in hopes I might see Him again and hear Him speak. And two men dressed in white dropped down by our sides and stood there and said: "Ye men of Galilee, why stand ye gazing into heaven? This same Jesus which is taken up from you into heaven, shall come in like manner as ye have seen Him go into heaven."'"

Then Mr. Moody said, "My friends, I want to ask you this question: Do you believe that picture is overdrawn? Do you believe Peter had

Paul as his guest and didn't take him to Gethsemane, didn't take him to Calvary and Mount Olivet? I myself spent eight days in Jerusalem, and every morning I wanted to steal down into the garden where my Lord sweat great drops of blood. Every day I climbed Mount Olivet and looked up into the blue sky where He went to His Father.

"I have no doubt Peter took Paul out on those three walks. If there had been a man that could have taken me to the very spot where the Master sweat those great drops of blood, do you think I would not have asked him to take me there? Now, you ministers, don't you believe the people want preaching like that? They do. They want to hear about the Lord."

I remember that I was sitting in that convention where I could easily see the faces of the people. It was a sight not to be forgotten. I remember that sea of eager upturned faces as distinctly as I remember Mr. Moody's talk. The people sat so still, as though in a spell, with eyes big and shining with something wet, and occasionally a slight twitching of emotion and a handkerchief called into service.

Mr. Moody talked in that natural way of his, so quiet and yet so intense in its quietness. That's what people want—Jesus brought to them, simply and naturally. And Moody knew it. It took years of hard self-discipline for him to be able to talk as he did. Such talking takes study and hard work. But it's all worth while if we can make

Jesus

Jesus plain to men in all His wondrous winsomeness.

"*A More Excellent Way.*"

Then there's another way of telling the story of Jesus to men. It's a yet better way. *Tell it with your life.* That was Jesus' own plan. He lived what He taught. He proposed coming down into each one of us and living His life over again in us. He does just that now. Then as men meet us they are meeting Him, too, in us. The things that marked Him will be noticed in us.

The intense hatred of sin, the purity, the gentleness and patience, the warm sympathy, the constant self-forgetfulness and self-sacrifice, the eagerness to win men, the tireless going wherever men could be helped—these may be in us as they were in Him, and will be, as we let Him live in us. And men will recognize the Jesus-story being lived in their midst. Jesus wants to reach out through us to men. And He will; He will; more than we ever know or will know. This is the best telling of the story.

I am told that in the Palace of Justice in Rome there is a remarkable chamber where visitors are sometimes taken. The remarkable thing about it is the decorations. The ceiling and walls and even the floors are covered with strangely painted frescoes. That is, they seem strange as one enters. They seem grotesque. They do not harmonize. They are out of touch with each other, and make a bewildering maze of confusion.

But there is one spot in the chamber, just one spot upon the floor, where, if you stand, everything falls into place. The artist's conception stands out perfect in perspective and color and beauty.

To the great crowd of men in this old world life seems a good bit like that Roman chamber. Things seem out of harmony—sin, pain, confusion, unsatisfied longings, unconquered weaknesses, broken plans, and disappointed ambitions. But there is one spot, a central point, just one, where all that concerns you will come into harmony, and bring heart-rest.

That one spot is where you take your stand side by side with Jesus. His presence clears everything up. He sweetens the life, and straightens the path, and leads you steadily on toward the dawning of the day. And that's as true for China and the Pacific islanders as for Britisher or American. Men need Jesus. He satisfies them. He is the great magnet. He draws men as no other can. He places Himself at our disposal to be taken to men. They can't resist Him. Let us take Him.

O Jesus Master, thou hast drawn me till I want to be Thy slave forever. Help me take Thee to all other men that they may feel Thy wondrous drawing power, and satisfying power, too.

THE HOLY SPIRIT

The Last Talk Together.
The Partnership of Service.
The Power That Never Fails.
The Trinity of Service.
Living on the Top Floor.
Partial Weavings of the Strands.
Unbroken Connection Above.

The Holy Spirit

The Last Talk Together.

A little group of men were climbing the winding path that led up Olivet's slope. The Master was in the midst, and the others before and behind, where they could hear His voice. For they were talking together as they walked along. That is to say, He was talking, and they were listening, with an occasional question. They went on until they were over against where little Bethany nestles in among the blue hills. There they stood a little while, still talking together earnestly.

It was their last talk together. And there were two things the Master was saying. Those two things came with all the tender emphasis of a last message. They were to go on an errand to the world; a lifelong errand, and to the whole world. That was being burned in. But they weren't to start on the errand until the Holy Spirit had come upon them. The errand and the Spirit's presence were coupled together. That was to be their errand. And He was to be their life-power as they went on the errand.

They were to go. The Spirit was to come. He would come before they went. They must not go until He had come. Then they were to go in His presence and power. They would be able to go because of Him. Their going would be worth while, because wherever they went He would be at work in them and through them. The real work would be done by Him. But it would be done through them. His presence was essential to their work being done. Their presence was essential to His doing His work. He would work as they went, and where they went.

That was the new blessed partnership of world-wide service planned by the Master as He went away. They would tell of Jesus. The Spirit would open doors, guide their tongues, guard their persons, and make the message of Jesus as a flame of fire in men's hearts.

Just before this, Jesus had talked a great deal with His disciples about the Holy Spirit. They didn't yet know how much this that He was saying, would come to mean to them. But they remembered after the Master was gone, and then they understood. When they got down into the thick of the world's crowds they understood the great significance of what He had said.

That last talk[1] they had together in the upper room and along the Jerusalem streets, on the betrayal night, was full of teaching about the Holy Spirit. And the next time after that that they met; in the upper room,[2] on the evening of the resurrection day, He breathed strongly upon them, and said, "Receive ye the Holy Spirit." And the very

[1] John, chapters 14-16. [2] John 20:19-23.

The Holy Spirit

last word on the Olivet slope was, "Wait; wait until the Holy Spirit comes." He burned in deep that their dependence must be entirely upon the Spirit.

The Partnership of Service.

Jesus Himself is an illustration of what He told them about this. He was on a missionary errand. He had been sent by His Father, even as later these men and we have been sent. With awe ever growing, one remembers that the divine Jesus in the days of His humanity gave Himself over to the control of the Holy Spirit. The Spirit was the dominant factor in His life and in all His activities. All His teachings and movements were at the suggestion and direction and control of the Spirit. The power in speech and action, in healing, in raising the dead, and in the wondrous mastery of Himself was the Holy Spirit's power working upon and through Jesus.

Then it was that as He was going away He said, "As the Father hath sent me, even so I send you." And with that He coupled the significant breathing upon them, with the word, "Take ye the Holy Spirit." We are to be as He, both in our utter dependence upon the Spirit and in our assurance of His power in us.

Ever since then that has been the effective partnership for world-service: men and the Holy Spirit; the Holy Spirit and men. If you are thinking of the human side you say, "*Men* and the Holy Spirit." If you are speaking of the divine side, you say, "*The Holy Spirit* and men." The two belong together. Where men have failed to go the Spirit has been hampered in speaking to men. He has spoken, but the story of salvation through Jesus has not been known. The Spirit's mouthpiece for the telling of that story was lacking. That seriously hindered Him in His work.

Where men have gone without the Spirit, that is without yielding themselves habitually to His control, they have been sorely hampered. It is like having the kindling wood set in order for a fire, but the fire not started. There is no heat, nor any of fire's results. The kindling must have the flame, and the flame must have the coals. The two are partners in service.

This partnership belongs peculiarly in the worldwide service of winning men. If anybody needs the Spirit's presence, he does who attempts to win a man to Jesus anywhere. But if any manwinner needs that presence more than another, he does who goes into the peculiar atmosphere of a non-Christian people. And, on the other hand, if anybody can be sure of the Spirit's presence and power always with him, and working through him, he can who has gone out on the world-errand.

That man is in the direct line of obedience to Jesus' command. The Spirit Himself is sent by Jesus, and comes to us in direct obedience to Jesus' desire. These two, the man and the Spirit, are as one in the purpose that controls them. That man may depend on the gracious, irresistible Spirit's power at every turn. He is a thrice blest

The Holy Spirit

man, if he have learned to depend upon His unseen Partner.

The Power That Never Fails.

You and I have to remind ourselves constantly that our chief dependence is not upon organization, nor method, nor personal talent, nor personal training, but upon the Holy Spirit working *through* these. The better organized the human machinery, the better the methods used, the more there is of personal gift, and the more thoroughly one's powers have been drilled, the more there is at the Spirit's disposal for Him to use. The practical bother is to remember this; to get it rubbed in until it is like an instinct in us, that the power is all from Him, through us. Not without Him, and not without us; the two together; but always His the far greater part—indeed, the real part.

The Holy Spirit has a double work to do: with us who go; and upon those to whom we go. Within us He has to work out the character of Jesus. He opens the Word, making its meaning stand clearly out. He wakens the mind up to do its best work. He guides in our decisions, suggesting and directing and controlling our thoughts, and in our actions, in our dealings with men. In things that are little in themselves, but on which so much hinges, He guides.

It constantly occurs that we are not at all conscious of His control at the time. But afterward we can see how He has been deftly, softly guiding, with His rare light touch upon us. When, in the thick of work, we may be pressed hard, and a bit wearied, and in doubt, He sends the quiet, quick suggestion into our thoughts that leads out of the tight corner and into the achievement of the thing desired. He works through us, and through what we do, giving power that otherwise would not be there. While you are talking in conversation or in public address, He is working through what you are saying.

And He works upon those to whom we go. He opens doors; the doors of circumstances that we find locked and double-padlocked against us. He opens the yet tighter-shut, harder-to-open human doors. He inclines men favorably toward us personally, and to our message. Under His touch the message becomes as a tongue of flame, kindling, disturbing, softening, burning down, and moulding over into new shape the inner man to whom the message comes.

Sometimes quarrymen find a very hard kind of rock in the stone quarries. They pick little grooves for the iron wedges, and then with great sledge-hammers drive these wedges into the hard rock. But sometimes this fails to split the rock. The iron wedges and big sledges have no effect at all on the stubborn stone. Then they go at it in another way. The iron wedges are removed from the narrow grooves. Then little wooden ones, of a very hard fibre are selected. These sharp-edged, well-made wooden wedges are first soaked in water. Then they are put in the grooves tightly while wet, and water is kept in the grooves. The sledges are not used. They would smash the wooden wedges.

The water and wedges are left to do their work. The damp wood swells. The particles must have more room as they swell. The granite heart of rock can't stand against this new pressure. It takes longer than with iron wedges and sledge, but after a while the rock yields and lies split wide-open. The water works on the wood, and that in turn on the stone. The iron wedges sometimes fail, but the wood and water never fail.

It seems to be a part of our make-up to make plans, and to count on the plans. And planning does much. We don't want to plan less, necessarily, but to learn to depend more *in* our planning on the soft, noiseless, but resistless power of the Holy Spirit.

"The day is long, and the day is hard;
We are tired of the march and of keeping guard;
Tired of the sense of a fight to be won,
Of days to live through, and of work to be done;
Tired of ourselves and of being alone:
Yet all the while, did we only see,
We walk in the Lord's own company.
We fight, but 'tis He who nerves our arm;
He turns the arrows that else might harm,
And out of the storm He brings a calm;
And the work that we count so hard to do,
He makes it easy, for He works, too:
And the days that seem long to live are His—
A bit of His bright eternities—and close to our need
  His helping is."[1]

[1] Susan Coolidge.

The Trinity of Service.

Now, we want to mark keenly that *full* power depends upon three things. There is a trinity of service, a human-divine trinity. The full results can come only through its working. The ideal winner of men needs to believe thoroughly in this trinity.

First of all is *the message*. There needs to be a clear understanding of the Gospel. That is the winner's message. That is the direct thing he uses in approaching and laying siege to some man's heart. It is a simple message, but very often it is grasped only partly by those who tell it.

That message needs to be understood clearly and fully by the man who would have the greatest power in winning men. From its first plain teaching about sin, on to the terrible results that sin left to itself works out; through the blessed teaching of love as shown most in the sacrifice for sin which Jesus made on the cross; the need of a clean cutting with sin, and clear-out surrender to Jesus as Saviour and Master; the work of the Holy Spirit in one's heart; and then the climax of service out among men—this simple message needs to be grasped fully and clearly. This is the first great essential in the trinity of service.

There is a second thing, yet more important, that must go with this first. And that is *a man who embodies the message* in himself. It isn't enough to know the story of the Gospel, nor to tell

The Holy Spirit

it. It must be *lived*. That is the best telling of it. The man must be a living illustration of the truth he is telling. He may be conscious of not illustrating it as he should. The earnest man is never aware that he is as good an illustration of it as he is. He may think himself a poor illustration. He is quite apt to. But he is yet more apt not to be thinking of that side as he attempts to win men. He will be all taken up with Jesus, and with getting men to know Him.

The man is more than the message, even when he is less than the message. When his life fails to live out the truth he is speaking, still even then he is more. For the life is more than the lips. And, while he is talking, his life is discounting his words and taking away some of the power that belongs with them. I do not mean that those he is talking to are making the comparison, necessarily. They may not know about his life, whether it embodies the message or not.

I mean that the life that is true breathes a force and power into the man himself and so into his words. *Or* it doesn't. The message takes on the quality of the man. One man's talking catches fire; another's doesn't. The listeners know that it is so, though they don't usually know why. All the while you and I are trying to win others, in Sunday-school class or meeting, in Gospel service or church preaching, in personal conversation or letter-writing, there's a subtle something that goes out of us, as an atmosphere, that affects the power of the message we're giving out.

And that something is actually greater in its power than the truth we are speaking. It may be a touch of flame making the truth burn within him who is listening. It may be a deadly, dampening chill checking the fire that is naturally in the truth. The man is always more than the message.

Living on the Top Floor.

Then there is a third thing. It is yet more than the message or the man, or than both message and man together. It is this: *the Holy Spirit controlling the man who embodies the message.* I mean by controlling him that he has surrendered himself to the Spirit's control. And, further than that, that he cultivates the Spirit's presence.

There needs to be a habitual cultivation of the Spirit's presence and friendship, even as we cultivate our human friendships. There needs to be time spent alone, habitually, with the Book of God. I do not mean just now merely studying the Bible to get better acquainted with its contents. Something more than that—thoughtful meditation on its truths; the quiet, steady holding of one's self open to the searching and stimulating and enlightening influence of this rare Book. The Spirit speaks through these pages. Yet it is to be feared that many a careful student of its pages does not get deeper in than the print. He doesn't know and meet the Person who speaks in the print and through it.

Then, beyond the quiet time with the Book,

The Holy Spirit

there is the holding of one's whole life open to the Spirit's suggestion and subject to His direction. He guides through our thinking. *And* sometimes He guides us when our thinking, for some reason, has not gotten up high enough for Him to guide through it. Samuel thought that David's oldest brother was God's chosen one. But into his rarely sensitized inner ear the Spirit said "No." His thinking wasn't keen enough to be the channel through which he could be guided. But he had learned to hold his thinking subject to a higher power.

One time Paul thought it would be good to go over east into the province of Bithynia, and even tried to make a start that way. But the Spirit made plain His plan that they were to go in just the opposite direction, to the west. Had Paul's thinking been more open to the Spirit's touch at that point, he wouldn't have made the false start. But he was wise clear beyond the great crowd of us. For at once he dropped his own thought-out plans, and did as he was bid.

The keener our mental processes are, the better informed we are, the better poised our judgment—the better can the Spirit reveal His plans to us through this natural channel, if it is open to Him. But there is one thing higher up than our thinking powers. And that is the spirit-perception. The mental isn't at the top. It's a step up to the spirit floor, the highest of all.

Some men of splendid ability and training and consecration are constantly hampered because they insist on living on the mental floor. All their decisions are made there, *not* subject to change from above. And the Holy Spirit, who is the Commander-in-chief of all the forces in this campaign, is unable to use them as He would.

They haven't got the sensitized inner ear of the quiet time that would lead them up into higher, broader service. They go faithfully plodding along on the lower level. The Spirit can use them, of course. He does; but never to the full. The Spirit of God controlling the man who embodies the message—this brings fulness of power in winsome service; and only this can. It is not by keenness of thinking, nor fulness of learning, nor shrewd, well-balanced judgment, but by the Spirit of God working through these, and sometimes working higher up than they have reached.

Partial Weavings of the Strands.

Now it will help us, I am sure, and make the truth stand out more clearly, to recall a good many variations that belong in here. Running back over these things brings up certain facts.

The truth has power of blessing in itself, regardless of who is speaking it. A bad man may preach the Gospel, and the truth itself will be felt in spite of the man. There is a life in truth itself, quite apart from the medium of its transmission. This explains why men who have turned out to be bad men have had good results attending their ministry. But it was the truth making itself

The Holy Spirit

felt in spite of the handicap it suffered at the hands of the man talking.

And men whose understanding of the truth is very one-sided and meagre have been greatly used and blessed in their work. It is striking how a man who has been rescued from a life of open sin, and who goes into Christian service with tremendous earnestness, will have great power. His emphasis of truth may be one-sided. It is quite apt to be. He tells what he has experienced. The man himself is a living illustration of the truth spoken. All the truth that can get out through him has the tremendous push forward of his life. But the extent of his service is limited.

And there are men who have a clear, well-rounded grasp of the blessed message of Jesus, and who give it out clearly and fully. But they are hampered by their mental swaddling-clothes, in which they have been wrapped up in schooldays. They never get up out of them into the freedom of strong action through the Spirit's control.

Then, too, without doubt God's Spirit works alone, without using anybody. He speaks through nature's beauty and power. He speaks in the inner heart of every man. He is speaking directly to men all the time everywhere. But the message is a partial one. The direct revelation of God, in nature and in conscience, is a limited revelation. The full revelation of God was made in Jesus. And so it is in this Book that tells of Jesus.

The Spirit of God can speak most fully where that Book is known. He can work most fully and powerfully through the man who lives the Book. Every printing of this Bible, or any part of it, is giving the spirit freer entrance into men's hearts. Every one of us who produces a new translation of it in the language of his life gives the Spirit a wide-open door where otherwise the opening had been narrow.

Now, whatever combination of these there may be, some of the blessed power of God will be seen and felt. The truth unembodied or even hampered; men who embody the truth they know, but whose knowledge is small; men of much knowledge, but small practice; men of full knowledge, but who have not learned to let the Spirit sway them fully; the Spirit Himself speaking where Jesus is not known, and without any man's help—through each of these, power of life will go out to men.

But the fulness of power that runs like a mighty stream goes only as the three things come into one. The *message*, full and clear, the *man* who lives it, the *Holy Spirit possessing and controlling the man* who lives the message—this is the trinity of service through which alone the flood-tide flows.

Unbroken Connection Above.

That blessed flood-tide of power may be much more common than it is. There needs to be daily quiet time, alone with the Master, with the door

The Holy Spirit

shut, the Book open, the knee bent, the will bent too, to a clear right angle, the mind quiet and open, the inner spirit unhurried; broad, thoughtful reading; keen, clear, quiet meditation; the rigorous squaring of the life up to the standard of the Book; the cultivation of the Spirit's presence and friendship; and these habits steadily followed until they become second nature.

Then will be fulfilled the promise, "Out of His inner being *shall flow rivers of water of life.*"[1] And men have always been drawn irresistibly to the rivers. And yet, while there will be fulness of power, there will not be full knowledge of how full the power is. That is reserved for "the Morning."

For hundreds of years men have used a contrivance called a diving-bell for working under water. Practically it enables a man to live out of his native element. For a man to live in water for any length of time is impossible. Expert divers do so for a few minutes at a time, but must rise constantly to get a fresh supply of air. But their work is dangerous, and very trying on the body. By means of the diving-bell a man may live and work for hours under the water; that is to say, in an element that of itself, unchecked, would quickly take his life.

The diving-bell is a sort of huge inverted cup, let down into the water by its own weight, opening downward, so that the man in the bell faces the water directly with nothing between himself

[1] John 7:38.

and it. Death by drowning is always within arm's length, yet he remains safe. The simple principle on which the thing is constructed is that water and air can't occupy the same space at the same time. The bell, being full of air, holds the water out.

But there needs to be a continual supply of fresh air sent down by means of a tube connected with the upper air. Death by drowning and death by suffocation, both threaten constantly, and each is held off, one by the air, and the other by the continual supply of fresh air. The man's ability to work and his very life depend upon the uninterrupted connection with the fresh air above.

The Christian man in this world is living out of his native breathing element. He needs to have his own atmosphere with him, or else he will die. And he needs to have a fresh supply continually from above, or his life will be at very low ebb.

Missionaries in foreign-mission lands speak much of the peculiar, deadening, moral atmosphere there. There is a strange sense of depression in it. They always plan to have their children brought home at an early age that they may be brought up through the tender, impressionable years in a land where Christian standards of life are recognized.

There is no language strong enough to put this truth, that we *must*, each of us, whether here or there, carry our own atmosphere with us, and have continual uninterrupted connection with the upper air. And that *"must"* cannot be too strongly underscored.

Blessed Holy Spirit, breath of God, and breath of my life, help me to let Thee have full sweep within me, that so my life may be kept sweet and full; and so Jesus can get freely and fully out of me to the great hungry crowd.

PRAYER

The Greatest Doing Is Praying.
At The Other End.
A Weekly Journey round the World.
Prayer a Habit.
A Praying Bent of Mind.
The Man Is the Prayer.
Unseen Changes Going On.

Prayer

The Greatest Doing Is Praying.

THE greatest of all things we can *do* is to *pray*. Jesus lived a life of prayer. All that He did and said grew out of His prayer. There is no way of knowing exactly how far it was so. But the more I study His life the stronger grows the impression that His teaching and activity, which form the greater part of these Gospel pages, were actually less than His praying. He seems to have put prayer first. All the rest was an outgrowth of it. He was on a world-winning errand. And this was what He thought of prayer. *The emphasis of Jesus' personal habit was laid upon prayer.*

The Holy Spirit is a prayer-spirit. He is the Master-Intercessor. He breathes into us the spirit of prayer, and makes it glow into a passion. He teaches us how to pray. It is a lifelong teaching. You who are teachers know that patience and skill are more in a good teacher than the knowledge taught. With greatest skill, and loving, tactful patience the Spirit teaches us to pray.

And then He does more: He uses each of us as

His praying-room, praying in us with yearnings beyond utterance the prayer to which we have not yet reached up, but which needs to be prayed down on the earth. All the power needed in this great winning work is in the Holy Spirit and comes from Him. *And the chief thing He emphasizes is prayer.*

The greatest thing each one of us can do is to pray. If we can go personally to some distant land, still we have gone to only one place. But our field is the world. It is impossible for us to reach our whole field personally. But it can be reached, and reached effectually, by prayer. The place where you and I are sent, whether at home or abroad, is simply our *base of action*. It is our field for *personal* touch. And that means very much. But it is more than that. It is only a small part of our field of activity. It is most significant as our *base of action*, from which we send out our secret messengers of prayer to all parts of the field.

And then, in the particular town or city or country district to which we have been sent, or in which we are being kept, the prayer properly comes before the personal activity. And it runs along side by side with the activity, and follows along after. We give the personal touch which must be given, and which may be so marvellous in power, but there's something even there greater than the great personal touch; and that is the power of prayer.

It is through the prayer that the personal presence means most. That personal presence may become a positive hindrance. It may be a drag upon the work. It often is just that for lack of prayer. For the real sweetness and efficiency of personal service out among men is in secret prayer.

And if we give *money*, it needs even more the prayer to go with it. Money seems almost almighty. As a winning force, of course, it must be reckoned far less than personal service. For it is less. It gets its almost omnipotence from human hands. If the personal touch depends for its subtle power on prayer, how much more does money! Money given to missions, unaccompanied by prayer, can no doubt be made to do great good. But it is a very pauper in its poverty alongside the bit of money that is charged with the spirit-current of prayer.

At the Other End.

One day I ran across a party of about twenty Pittsburg men on their way to a men's Christian convention in Cincinnati. There were a few ministers in the party, but it was made up chiefly of business men, typical, keen, alert American business men. We got together and talked about things of common interest.

And this question was asked: *Does prayer do things?* Then the question was spread out some. I go into my room at night to retire. I read a bit from the Book, and kneel to pray. I pray for a man in Pittsburg or in Hang-chow, China. Does anything take place in Pittsburg or in Hang-chow that wouldn't have taken place if I hadn't prayed? Of course, the praying does *me* good. The very bending of knee and head before God, the good wishes in my heart going out to some one else—these influence me. I rise better for both.

But is that all? Does anything happen *at the other end?* Does my prayer do anything in Hang-chow? If I write a business letter to Hang-chow, enclosing a foreign draft, the letter does something. A vast amount of business is carried on that way. Would the prayer as really do something as the letter and the draft?

There was a good bit of talk back and forth, and questions asked. It was interesting to find these men were ready to admit that they really believed that something would occur at the other end. They belonged to a church noted for its sound teaching, and came from the orthodox church city of Pittsburg. The matter-of-fact power of prayer to do business "at the other end" seemed to appeal to these business men. Apparently they had not been looking at prayer that way. But they readily admitted that it must be so. Then the next question asked itself: How much of this foreign business are we doing? And so the little crowd talked along while the train pounded the rails at the rate of forty-odd miles an hour.

Prayer does do things. Something happens at the other end that wouldn't happen if the prayer were not made. The banker can touch London and Paris and Shanghai and Calcutta and Tokyo, without moving from the desk where he is dictating letters, with his correspondence spread out before him. The praying man can as really touch these cities as he kneels in his room, with map and Book spread out before him.

Things are changed out there that need changing. That banker does business, too, in his home city and out in the home-land. But many times, with many a house, the bulk of foreign business is in excess of that done at home. Now we want to do a large business abroad in soul-winning and in world-winning, as well as at home.

A Weekly Journey round the World.

I use that word "business" in this connection thoughtfully and reverently. I know there is a sacredness, a hallowedness about prayer that never or rarely enters into business matters. We keep the two things apart in our thoughts; reckoning the one a common thing, and the other a holy thing. And I would increase, if I could, that sense of reverence in prayer. But there is a great advantage in using the familiar language of business in thinking of the results of our praying.

Prayer is doing business for God. It gives a practicality, a something-you-can-touch-and-feel feeling to think in that way. Shall we not make plans at once to increase our foreign correspondence?

You can have a simple schedule or memorandum to guide your praying. I do not mean a slavish hard-and-fast system, or set of rules, set down to be followed, with a feeling that you have been untrue if you forget. Nothing of that sort at all. But merely a simple something to glance at each day, and so serve as a reminder to guide your thoughts.

A little memorandum can be made running through the days of the week. It can be so planned as to run around the world during the week. The little schedule which I use is divided into the days of the week, Sunday to Saturday. There is a daily page containing notes, catch-words, about personal affairs, and home, and friends, and church, and appointments, and such items. Then each day of the week has a page, and on it is marked home-land items and foreign items.

In marking out the weekly world journey I had to begin somewhere. The Master told the disciples to begin at Jerusalem and work out. So I followed that rule, and Sunday is marked Turkey and the lands grouped with it, Arabia and Persia. The memorandum moves east, following the compass-line of greatest need. Monday is India day, including Ceylon and the lands and islands lying adjacent. Tuesday is China day; Wednesday, Japan, the island kingdom; and the island world of the Pacific.

This brings me across the Pacific, and so Thursday is marked South America, including Central America and Mexico. The easterly line takes me across the Atlantic again to Africa on Friday. Saturday takes an upward turn to the papal lands of Europe, and to Russia, completing the world-journey for that week. The matters for prayer here in the home-land are noted through the days of the week in the same way. Each page has certain home and certain foreign items.

A little prayer-book of that sort grows under constant use. Your reading of missionary news leads to the making of fresh notes. Names of persons are added, and dates of coming conferences, and so on, and verses of Scripture that stand out in the daily reading. So the book becomes to you a very precious little batch of leaves, lying inside the precious Book of God.

It should be accompanied by a map of the world. For a good while I used the one which was inserted in one of Dr. A. T. Pierson's mission books. That copy has long since been replaced by others, larger, giving more information. It is an immense help to glance at the map daily, and look at the part marked for the day. The lands get fixed in mind in that way without special effort. Gradually they stand out more and more clearly, and come to be very real to you.

That map may become dear to you, for it suggests the field that you are influencing. It is your prayer sailing-chart. It becomes fragrant with memories. Experiences you have had alone with God over His Word, and over this map of His World, come back to refresh and sweeten.

Prayer A Habit.

There's a little sentence of Paul's that used to puzzle and bother me, "Pray without ceasing." But it has become a great help to me. It puzzled me because I didn't see any practical way of doing it. It didn't seem to mean the repetition of prayers, with little mechanical helps, such as some use. It surely doesn't mean staying on your knees a long time. But, as I tried to pray my way into its meaning, it came to mean four distinct things to me. And I would not be surprised to find more yet coming out of it.

First of all, it means that prayer should be *a habit*. There should be a fixed time every day, or times, for going off alone to pray. Into that time the Book is taken. Quiet time is spent in reading it. For this is listening to God. And that comes first in praying; listening first, then speaking. The reading may be rapid and broad, or slower and more meditative. Whichever it may be, there should be a cultivation of *the habit of meditation*.

I do not mean a sleepy trying to imitate what we suppose some holy men do. But a keen thinking into the meaning of the words, and into their practical use in one's own life. Then the praying itself. The being still before God, and the definite prayer for particular things, and persons, and places. That habit can be fixed until it becomes second nature. It can be cultivated until it becomes the sweet spot of the day to you.

Prayer

A Praying Bent of Mind.

Then while the daily habit continues prayer may become an attitude, *a bent of mind.* Whatever comes up suggests prayer to you. The bent of your mind is to pray as things come up in the daily round. You can't stop your work, but you *think* prayers. Your heart prays while your hands are busy.

I shall never forget the school in which I learned to pray this way. A case of protracted illness in my home required my personal attention constantly for a time. It seemed as if no assistance I could get meant quite as much as what I could do personally. The life in peril was so precious that all else dropped out of sight. My habits of life were completely broken up. I was up night and day. The early morning hour of reading and prayer was broken into, with everything else of a regular sort.

But as I went about my round of service I found myself praying constantly. I was much wearied, and things sometimes seemed desperate. I realized how everything depended on God's touch. And without any planning a habit of continual praying formed itself. I could be engaged in conversation, thinking intently into something needing great care, and yet there was an undercurrent of prayer constantly. I shall never cease to be grateful for that trying experience, because in it this new habit of a praying bent of mind formed itself.

Do you not know how as you go about your ordinary round there is a constant undercurrent of thought? You may be talking, or reading, or writing, or doing something more mechanical, and yet this underneath train of thought is running along apparently of its own accord, regardless of you. It is broken at times, or you lose consciousness of it, as your work requires closer attention. When you swing into the habitual things that you have done over and over again until they almost do themselves, it reasserts itself.

I remember years ago, in a banking-house where I served for a time, I had long additions to make. Sometimes the rows of figures to be added up were a foot in length. And I got so used to adding that often I was surprised to find that my thoughts had been far away, completely taken up with something else, while I had been adding the figures. And fearing that I had been slighting my work, I would go back carefully all over the figures, only to find the footings correct. The adding habit had become fixed, and left the undercurrent of my thought free.

That current is apt to reveal the heart's purpose or set of mind. Whatever you are most set upon, whatever your favorite fads or hobbies or inclinations or moods are, they are apt to appear in that involuntary train of thinking. Now this can be cultivated. It can be cultivated chiefly by the cultivation of the controlling purpose of your life, and then by trying to give directions to

Prayer

the undercurrent, and holding it to that direction. If Jesus has gripped your heart the purpose of the life will be for Him. And if you have come to realize the tremendous power of prayer, this undercurrent of thought can be made a prayer-current.

I do not mean by any forced or artificial holding of one's self to such a current by dint of main force, and then mentally whipping yourself if you have forgotten. The power of all action lies in its being perfectly free and natural. You can cultivate the Jesus-passion, and the life-purpose, and the prayer-habit, and all of this will be a training of that undercurrent of thought toward prayer.

The shipping clerk, as he heads up his barrels and boxes, can be sending out and up his current of prayer. At intervals he is thinking closely about something connected with his work. Then his thoughts free themselves. As he hammers in the nails, his thought says, "This is China day." Each ringing blow of the hammer rings out "This is China day:—Thy blessing, Master, to-day upon the missionaries in Hang-chow;—upon Mr. Blank out there;—victory in Jesus' name to-day; —the physician missionaries, the nurses;—Thy power upon them;—help the native workers."

The picture of his little prayer memorandum comes up before his mind's eye. The map of China stands out more or less distinctly, according to how long he may have been practising looking at it in his prayer-hour. His mind runs of itself from one point to another. And so, all the while, his undercurrent of praying goes on. It is broken into by newer or more exacting duties; then free again, and swinging more or less to the thing his heart is set upon. It becomes a perfectly free, natural thing with him. This is part of the meaning of "Pray without ceasing."

The Man is the Prayer.

Then prayer is *a life*. The life is what you are in yourself. It is not the mere span of years you live through. Your thoughts and loves, your heart's ambitions and gripping purposes, the things you will to do, and to be—that is your life. That exerts an enormous influence upon the circle in which you live, and upon the world.

If underneath all else that driving purpose, that warm, intense love-power, that yearning desire, is Godward, and manward, and worldward, that becomes a prayer, a continual prayer. You are not thinking of it that way. But that is your life, and that life is a prayer. Its influence against the evil one and for God is enormous.

That is a prayer unceasing, as long and as strong as your life itself. Satan fears it. It hinders him and thwarts him every day. The fragrant incense from the censer of your life rises up before the throne of God continually, and affects the events on the earth.[1]

And then prayer is *a person*. That is to say, you yourself may be a prayer, a walking prayer offered

[1] Revelation 8: 3–5.

Prayer

up in Jesus' name. Your presence will affect the evil one, and change events, and help God in His plans. You may be so allied with Jesus in the simple gripping purpose of your heart that you yourself, where you are, by your mere presence, will be recognized by evil spirits, and by the Master Himself as a mighty power for God.

Your presence disturbs the evil one's plan. It has an influence upon those you meet. It is helping God. The whole effect of your presence is precisely the same as a prayer. You are a prayer yourself, though unconsciously. The whole trend of your life says, "Thy Kingdom come; Thy will be done on earth as in heaven."

A few years ago President Roosevelt's daughter was a member of the Taft party that visited parts of the Orient. She did not go as the President's daughter, of course. There could be no official significance attached to her presence. We Americans can understand better than some others that she went simply as a young woman eager to see Japan and China, not as the President's daughter.

But everywhere she went in the Orient she was treated not merely as a member of the party, but as the daughter of the President of the United States. Presents were made to her, receptions tendered, and deference shown, because of her personal relation to her father. To the Orientals her presence stood for the head of our Government. They treated her in relation to him.

Even so it is with us Christians. The evil one

doesn't think of you and me for ourselves simply. He thinks of us in relation to the Jesus, who is his Victor. We stand to him down here for Jesus. He fears us as he fears Jesus. That is, he can be made to fear us, by our being true to our Lord.

The final purpose of prayer is to defeat Satan and to bring about God's will. And we do just that in our persons, by our presence; or we may. Prayer is a person. You are a prayer. The man himself becomes a tremendous prayer, offsetting evil influences, changing men and events, and helping God in His plans.

These last two, the life and the person, may be called unconscious prayer. The influence is constantly going out, though we are not aware of it. But it is great encouragement to recall that this prayer-power is going out of us constantly. And these two are not limited to the place where we are. They act as a momentum to every wish we breathe, and every spoken prayer we utter, sending these with renewed force out to the place involved. Spirit influence does not know anything about the limitations of distance.

Unseen Changes Going On.

All this praying makes a difference at the other end, the place toward which it is directed. Things in Tokyo are made different. The copy of a Gospel that some native in India is reading becomes a plainer book to him because of this praying. Your prayer is a spirit-force travelling instantly through the distance between you and the place you are praying for. And things occur that otherwise would not.

Opposition lessens. Difficulties give way. The road some man is travelling clears and brightens. The truth on the printed page stands out in bigger letters. The health renews. The sickness or weakness gives way to a new health and strength. The judgment steers a straight course. The purpose holds its anchor steady. The man rides the rough seas of temptation safely.

Things are happening. And they are happening because some scarcely noticed young fellow hammering a barrel-head and marking the shipping directions, and some typewriter chopping her machine, are praying in the quiet time, and are praying softly in the undercurrent of their scarcely thought-out thoughts.

> "Oh, if our ears were opened
>   To hear as angels do
> The Intercession-chorus
>   Arising full and true,
> We should hear it soft up-welling
>   In morning's pearly light;
> Through evening's shadows swelling
>   In grandly gathering might;
> The sultry silence filling
>   Of noontide's thunderous blow,
> And the solemn starlight thrilling
>   With ever-deepening flow.
>
> "We should hear it through the rushing
>   Of the city's restless roar,

And trace its gentle gushing
 O'er ocean's crystal floor;
We should hear it far up-floating
 Beneath the Orient moon,
And catch the golden noting
 From the busy Western noon;
And pine-robed heights would echo
 As the mystic chant up-floats,
And the sunny plain resounds again
 With the myriad mingling notes.

"There are hands too often weary
 With the business of the day,
With God-entrusted duties,
 Who are *toiling while they pray.*
They bear the golden vials,
 And the golden harps of praise,
Through all the daily trials,
 Through all the dusty ways.
These hands, so tired, so faithful,
 With odors sweet are filled,
And in the ministry of prayer
 Are wonderfully skilled.

"There are noble Christian workers,
 The men of faith and power,
The overcoming wrestlers
 Of many a midnight hour;
Prevailing princes with their God,
 Who will not be denied,
Who bring down showers of blessing
 To swell the rising tide.
The Prince of Darkness quaileth
 At their triumphant way,
Their fervent prayer availeth
 To sap his subtle sway.

"And evermore the Father
 Sends radiantly down

Prayer

All-marvellous responses,
   His ministers to crown;
The incense cloud returning
   As golden blessing-showers,
We in each drop discerning
   Some feeble prayer of ours,
Transmuted into wealth unpriced,
   By Him who giveth thus
The glory all to Jesus Christ,
   The gladness all to us!"[1]

[1] Frances Ridley Havergal.

MONEY

Limitations.

The Best Partnership.

Jesus' Teaching.

Be Your Own Executor.

Missing the Master's Meaning.

Money Talks.

Debts.

Rusty Money.

Are We True to Our Friend's Trust?

Money

Limitations.

MONEY seems almost almighty in its power to do things, and make changes. It can make a desert blossom as a rose. It can even defy death. Medical skill holds the life here that otherwise would have been snuffed out. Great buildings go up. Colleges begin their life with apparatus and books, skilled instructors, and eager students. Mammoth enterprises spring into being. Hospitals and churches rise up with skilled attendants and talented preachers.

We have come, in our day, and perhaps peculiarly in our country, to think that there is no limit to the power of money. Our ideas of its value are really greatly exaggerated. That first sentence I used would be revised by many to read, "Money is almighty." The cautious words "seems" and "almost" would be promptly cut out.

Yet money has great limitations. It will help greatly to remember what they are. And many of us need the brain-clearing of that help. Of itself money is utterly useless, so much deadweight stuff lying useless and helpless. It must have human hands to make it valuable. It gets its value from our conception of its value and from our use of it. It must have a human partner to be of any service at all.

In bad hands it becomes devilish in its badness. And I needn't put an "almost" in that sentence. It may be as a very demon, or as the arch-devil himself, as really as it may seem to be divine in its creative and changing power.

Then it is valuable only in this world, on the earth. At the line of death its value wholly ceases. Over that line it takes its place as a pauper. It is represented as being used for cobble stones in the streets of the new Jerusalem. Yet it would need to go through some hardening process to make it of any account at all as paving material.

We ought to remind ourselves of something else, too, that the crowd constantly forgets, and that we are tempted to forget when touched by the contagion of the crowd. And that is, that money is always less in its power than a strong, sweet, pure life. Maybe you think that comparison can't properly be made. You say that things so unlike can't be compared. But, whether consciously or intentionally or otherwise, that comparison is being made constantly in practical life, and most times to the advantage of money. Commonly the crowd reckons money more than character.

We do well to remind ourselves that its influence for good is always distinctly less than that of a life. To live a life pure and strong and wholesome in its ideals out among men is more than to be able to give money in any amount. To keep one's life up to such ideals in the heartless drive and competition of modern life means more than to extract large quantities of gold out of the mine of barter and trade, and to give some of it away.

And money is less than personal service. Great deference is paid to checks and subscriptions. The man who can draw a large check for some good object, and who may by dint of much dexterous handling be induced to write his name under some large figure, is treated with awe. But there's another man who stands higher up in the scale, and to whom hats should go farther off and more quickly. That is the strong man who gives personal service. There may be a blessed partnership between the man of money and the man of service. There often is. But he is an unfortunate man, to be pitied, who lets anything else crowd out of his life the privilege of giving some of his self out in personal service for others. These are some of gold's limitations.

The Best Partnership.

Give money good partners, and there is no end to what it can do. Let prayer and sacrifice and money form a life-partnership, and that first sentence can be revised, and greatly strengthened by the revision: Money *is* almost almighty. It gets all the good qualities of its partners as long as it stays in the partnership, on good working terms.

It isn't the head of the firm, however. Prayer

belongs in that place. It must direct. It is the prayer's touch with God that hallows the gold and gives to it some of God's omnipotence. Money is the working partner, best when hard at work, and famous for the amount of work it can do in obeying orders from the head of the house.

It gives a strange sense of awe to realize that the bit of money you hold in your hand can be used to *change a life*, aye, more, to change many lives. That money is yours to control. It came to you in exchange for your labor or your skill. It is yours, for the sweat of your brow or your brain is upon it. And now it can be sent out, and the result will be a life utterly changed, purified, and redeemed.

Through your partnership the money produces something greater than itself. And that changed life becomes the centre of a new power, changing other lives out to the far rim of an ever-widening circle. It may have cost you much. Some of your very life has gone out in the work that brought into your hands that bit of gold. It is red with your blood. And now, if you choose, it can be sent out and made to bring new life in to some one else. Life has gone from you in getting it, and life will come to another in your giving it out, under the blessed Master's transmuting touch.

Jesus' Teaching.

Jesus' teaching about money is startling. I mean that it stands in such utter contrast to the commonly accepted standards out in the world, and

Money 251

inside in the Church, that the contrast startles one sharply.

There are four passages in which His money teachings group, largely. There's the "Lay-not-up for-yourselves-treasure-upon-the-earth" bit in the sermon on the Mount;[1] with the still stronger phrase in the Luke parallel, "Sell that ye have, and give."[2] There is the incident of the earnest young man who was rich;[3] the parable of the wealthy farmer in Luke, twelfth chapter;[4] and the whole sixteenth chapter of Luke, with that great ninth verse, whose full meaning has been so little grasped. The truth taught in each of these is practically the same thing.

The Master is evidently talking about what a man has over and above his personal and family needs. It's a law of life, from Eden on, that a man should work to supply his daily needs and the needs of those dependent upon him. Just how much that word "needs" means each man settles for himself. It means different things at different times to the same man.

It is surprising how little it can be made to mean when the pinch comes, and yet a man have all actual necessities supplied. The man who would have his life count for most for the Master, and the Master's plan, thinks over that word prayerfully and sensibly with full regard to personal strength, and loved ones, and the future. What-

[1] Matthew 6:19–21. [2] Luke 12:33, 34.
[3] Matthew 19:16–29. Mark 10:17–31. Luke 18:18–30.
[4] Luke 12:13–21.

ever it may be made to mean, this teaching is plainly about what is left over after the needs are met.

Now, about that left-over amount the Master gives three easily understood rules, or bits of advice, or commands. First: *Don't treasure it up for the sake of having it.* If you do it is in danger, and you are in danger. It may be stolen. Every vault, and safe, and safety-deposit company, and lock, and key backs up that statement. Or it may be lost through rust or moths, the two things that threaten all inactivity. The stuff that isn't in use wears away. The wear of use can't compare with the wear of disuse or neglect.

Then *you* are in danger of your heart being affected. It will be wherever your treasure is. It may get locked up, and so dried up for lack of air or poisoned by bad air. The blood must have fresh air. The heart must have touch with men to keep its vigor. It may get all dried up with *things*, instead of keeping vigorous by touch with needy men. That's the twofold danger. That's the first thing Jesus says: Don't store it up, down here, in the ordinary way.

The second thing is this: *Store your surplus up.* Be careful of it. Keep strict tally. Let the books be well kept and balanced. Let no thoughtlessness nor carelessness nor thriftlessness get in. Store it up. But be careful where you store it. Keep it carefully guarded against the action of thieves and moths, and against the inaction of decaying, destroying rust. That is the second thing. Store it up carefully.

Money

Be Your Own Executor.

The third thing is this: *Store it up by means of exchange.* Keep it safe by giving it away. The whole value of money is in exchange. It must be kept moving. But, *but*—and the whole heart of the teaching is here—be very wary about your exchanges. Invest your money in *men*, wherever the need may be. All that you invest wisely in men is stored up against any violence or craftiness of thieves and any corroding of rust.

All that is not out in active use directly among men, for men, in Jesus' name, is in danger of being stolen, or of decaying, or of injuring you, or of being left behind, utterly worthless to you when you are through down here. Be your own executor.

Some years ago one of the religious papers of New York City told of the death of a maiden lady named Elizabeth Pellit. Her home was in the hall-room of a tenement-house, and at her death all her earthly possessions could be put into one common trunk. No executor or administrator was needed. Living in narrow circumstances, her friends thought she had denied herself all luxuries and even many comforts. But in the forty years of her Christian life she had been able to give over thirty thousand dollars to missionary work. She had supplied the money to send out and sustain one missionary in Salvador, and also for another who was to go out soon. She seemed to have grasped the meaning of the Master's teaching.

Good common sense comes in for free play here, both in adjusting one's personal and family schedule and in giving. Giving may be done foolishly, or not wisely. There is no place where there is more room for good sense in avoiding both the extreme of unwise giving and the other extreme of handicapping one's gifts.

It is a question of personal judgment how far to give money out directly and how far to invest some of it and use the income wholly in gifts. You may think that in some directions you can invest it better, and direct the income better than some organization. That is an important detail. But the chief thing is that the money itself is dedicated wholly for use out among needy men.

Now you will please mark keenly that in all this I am not talking about what I think about money. I am simply putting into plain talk Jesus' own teaching about it, in these four great passages.

Missing the Master's Meaning.

Christian men, generally, seem to have missed the meaning of Jesus' words. I think it due largely to the lack of teaching in the Church that world-evangelizing is a *first* obligation.

Recently a fire destroyed the home of a man of large wealth who lives some distance east of San Francisco. It was a beautiful palace, full of art treasures. The value of house and furnishings and the art collection was reckoned at about two million dollars. He is a Christian

Money

man, prominently identified with active Christian work, and reckoned a liberal giver. He has visited foreign-mission lands, and made special gifts to missions.

But his gifts to missions seem like a copper cent or a silver quarter given to a beggar in contrast with the two million dollars tied up for himself in the house that burned. Two millions stored up in a home, while many millions of men have lived and died in ignorance of the light and peace that comes with Jesus! Yet this man calls Jesus his Master, and sincerely, I have no doubt. And his Master said the one great thing was to tell all men of His love and death.

By no extension of the meaning of that word "need" could he be said to need a two-million-dollar home for himself and family. And there are other millions under the same man's control. It looks very much as if this good man had missed the meaning of Jesus' words. The criticism, however, must be first upon the Church and its leaders, with whose general trend of teaching this man is in accord. According to the Master's teaching, most of the money in his house, and stored up in other ways of the sort for himself, is being lost. Far more serious, the opportunity of investment in men is being lost. That money will be all loss to him when he reaches the line of departure over into the next sphere of life.

It is very difficult to use such an illustration from life. There is danger that the words will sound critical in a bad or unkind sense. I earnestly pray to be kept from that. You will know that I am talking to myself first of all; and speaking of this only to help. The bother is that this man is not an exception. Rather he represents the habit and standard of his generation.

I recall another Christian man as I speak, of large wealth, by inheritance and by dint of business keenness. His face showed plainly his fine Christian character. He gave liberally in many directions, sometimes very large sums. But he lived in a home whose value ran close to a half-million of dollars. When he died, full of years and honors, he left many millions to a son who does not inherit his father's generous hand with his wealth. Of course, the son didn't *need* the vast wealth.

And I wondered, silently, within my heart, how things looked to that man, as he slipped out of life up into the Master's presence, and looked down on the earth through the eyes of the One whose teaching we have been talking about. He could see China and India and Africa then as plainly as America.

How did the lost opportunity of laying up his treasure in the lives of men look to him then, I wondered. He was a good man. I saw him smile once, and his face seemed to shine as an angel's. I think probably no faithful friend had ever talked to him of the plain meaning of Jesus' words, and of world-winning being a *first* obligation. He hadn't been taught it from the pulpit. And he hadn't thought into it himself.

Money

Money Talks.

Many are losing a great opportunity of silently preaching Jesus to their fellows by their habit of giving. Two men were discussing the evidences of the Christian religion. The one was a Christian; the other not, and inclined to be sceptical. Arguments were freely exchanged. At last the sceptic, who was a blunt, out-spoken man, said frankly, to his friend and neighbor: "I think we might as well drop this matter. For I don't believe a word you say. And, more than that, I am quite satisfied in my own mind that you do not really believe it yourself. For to my certain knowledge you have not given, the last twenty years, as much for the spread of Christianity, such as the building of churches and foreign and domestic missions, as your last Durham cow cost. Why, sir, if I believed what you say you believe I'd make the church my rule for giving, my farm the exception."

That Christian man's life was contradicting every word he uttered to his neighbor. Money talks. His was talking very loudly to his sceptical neighbor. His neighbor was unusually frank in saying out what thousands are thinking. He had lost a great opportunity of winning his friend.

Debts.

In a simple little sentence Paul reveals how thoroughly he had grasped Jesus' meaning. He said, "*I am debtor* both to Greeks and barbarians"—to all men.[1] Now that word, "debtor," commonly means two things: that you have received something of value from some one, and that therefore you owe him for what he gave to you.

But Paul hadn't gotten anything special from the men of whom he is speaking. His birth and training and whatever else he had were Jewish. And the Jews were a minority in the world. He was not under the debtor obligation of having gotten something from the men he is speaking of.

In his use of that word, "debtor" means *three* things: first, something received from God, and that something everything; then something owing to God; and then that something *payable to man*. He counted himself in debt to all men on Jesus' account. And so are we. How much owest *thou* to thy Lord? That's how much you are to pay to men on your Lord's account.

We are not even our own, much less our goods. We were bought up when we were bankrupt. A great price was paid for us, even the life-blood of Jesus. And our Owner bids us pay *up* by paying *out*. We are badly and blessedly in debt; badly, for we can never square the account; blessedly, because we can be constantly paying on account, out to men in Jesus' name.

> "Over against the Treasury this day
>   The Master silent sits; whilst, unaware
>   Of that Celestial Presence still and fair,
> The people pass or pause upon their way.

[1] Romans 1:14.

And some go laden with His treasures sweet,
   And dressed in costly robes of His device
   To cover hearts of stone and souls of ice,
Which bear no token to the Master's feet.

And some pass, gaily singing, to and fro,
   And cast a careless gift before His face,
   Amongst the treasures of the holy place,
But kneel to crave no blessing ere they go.

And some are travel-worn, their eyes are dim,
   They touch His shining vesture as they pass,
   But see not—even darkly through a glass—
How sweet might be their trembling gifts to Him.

And still the hours roll on; serene and fair
   The Master keeps his watch, but who can tell
   The thoughts that in His tender spirit swell,
As one by one we pass him unaware?

For this is He who, on one awful day,
   Cast down for us a price so vast and dread,
   That He was left for our sakes bare and dead,
Having given Himself our mighty debt to pay!

Oh, shall unworthy gifts once more be thrown
   Into His treasury—by whose death we live?
   Or shall we now embrace His cross, and give
Ourselves, and all we have, to him alone?"

Is not that the meaning of Paul's "Owe no man anything, save to love one another."[1] We owe a debt of love to all men on Jesus' account. We can be paying on it continually, and yet never get a receipt in full that discharges the debt. But then we get other things in full—peace, and joy, and a life overflowing in fulness.

[1] Romans 13:8.

With an honorable business man *a debt is a first obligation*. His personal expenditures and his home schedule are shaped by his debt. The extras that he would feel quite free in allowing himself and his home are not allowed until the debt is cleared. The debt controls his spendings until it is paid off in full. That's reckoned a matter of honor.

Rusty Money.

James, the first bishop of Jerusalem, had caught the Lord's very language as well as His thought. He says, "Your gold and silver are rusted, and their rust shall be for a testimony against you."[1] It would seem as though there were quite a bit of rusty money entered in Christian names and controlled by Christian people. It is lying in vaults, and lands, and savings-societies, and old stockings, gathering rust.

It is in sore need. It needs friction, the friction of use. Without that its real, rare value will be completely lost. It is furnishing food for moths when it was meant to be furnishing food for men, bread of wheat and bread of life. There'll be many a striking scene when some men come up into the Master's presence with loaded purses, "caught with the goods," while millions of their brothers are living such pitiable lives because of their ignorance of Jesus.

But there are men who do understand. And their number is increasing. There are those who understand *the Master's basis* for conducting their

[1] James 5:2, 3.

business matters. That basis is shrewd, faithful management of the business itself as good stewards of God; full, proper provision for home and loved ones—simple, but ample and intelligent; and then all the rest out in active service for men in Jesus' name. If that basis were more largely understood and accepted, what wondrous changes would come; changes out in the world, and changes in the home, and changes in the home church.

Many men are supporting their own representatives in the foreign field. Many a church now sustains its own missionary or missionaries. The ideal toward which the Church might well aim is that *every family* should have its own missionary. The real unit of life is the family. The children would then grow up with the world-vision clearly and deeply marked. There are thousands of families in circumstances that are reckoned moderate that could support a missionary by planning. But the relationship should be carefully kept one of warm sympathy and prayer, as well as one of money. The reflex blessing upon the home would be immeasurable in its sweetness and extent.

Are We True To Our Friend's Trust?

Jesus admits us into the inner circle of friendship. He gives us the one rarest token of friendship, that is, a task to do for our Friend's sake. He asks us to go out to all men, and tell them about His love and sacrifice for them. And He asks that everything we have be held and used for

Sacrifice

One Hank Over For the Candle.

The light of a common candle in the window of a little cottage near the coast shone far out over the sea. It was up north of Scotland, in one of the Orkney Islands. Near the window sat a frail, gray-haired woman with cheery, thoughtful face. She was busy working at her spinning-wheel, and watching the candle, turning now and again to trim it. All night long she sat at the spinning-wheel and watching the candle. Fishermen out on the water, heading for home, knew that light could be counted on, and came safely in, past all the dangers of their coast.

For more than fifty years that woman tended her little lighthouse. When she was a young girl there had been a wild storm, and her father, out in his fisherman's boat, lost his life. There were no shore-lights. His boat had struck a huge, dangerous rock called Lonely Rock, and been wrecked. The father's body was found in the morning washed up on the shore. She watched by her father's body, as was the habit of her people, until it was laid away. Then she laid down on her bed and slept the day through. When night came she rose, lit a candle, put it in the window, drew up her spinning-wheel, and began her night vigil for the unknown out at sea.

All night long, and all her life long, her vigil of love and light continued. From youth to old age, through winter and summer, storm and calm, fog and clear, that humble lighthouse beacon failed not. Each night she spun so many hanks of yarn for her daily bread, and *one hank over for the candle*. She turned night into day, reversing the whole habit of her life, and holding every other thing subject to her self-imposed task of love. And through the years many a fisherman out at sea, and many an anxious woman watching by hearth and crib, sent up heart-felt thanks to God for that little, steady light. And many a life was saved, of which no record could be kept.

That tells the whole story of sacrifice. A need, nobody to meet it; the need passing into an emergency; and that into the tragedy of an unmet emergency; a heart sore torn to bleeding by the tragedy thrust bitterly home; then sacrifice, life-long, that others might be saved where her loved one was lost, and still others spared what she herself suffered. And that story has been repeated with endless variations, and is being repeated, in every land, on every mission-field, home and foreign, and in almost every home of all the world.

Sin's Healing Shadow.

Sacrifice has come to be a law of life. Wherever there is sin there will be a *call for sacrifice.* For sin makes need, and need intensifies into emergency. And need and emergency mean sacrifice thrust upon some one in peril. And they call for sacrifice, volunteered by some one, who would save the man in peril. And wherever there are true men and women, as well as need, there will *be* sacrifice.

And sin is everywhere. Even nature is full of evidence of a bad break in all of its processes. The finger-marks of decay and death are below and above and all around in all its domain. That is sin's unmistakable ear-mark. Man's mental powers, and his loss of a full knowledge of his powers, tell the same story. And so there is need. Everywhere you turn need's pathetic face, drawn and white, looks piteously into yours, pleading mutely for help.

And so there is sacrifice. Sacrifice is sin's healing shadow. It follows sin at every turn, binding up its wounds, pouring in the oil and wine of its own life, and taking the hurt victims into its own warm heart. Nothing worth while has ever been done without sacrifice. Every good thing done cost somebody his life. The life was given out with a wrench under some sharp tug. Or it was given in the slower, more painful, more taxing way of being lingeringly given out through years of steadfast doing or enduring.

Every man who has done something worth while for others has spilled some of his life-blood into it. His work and name may have become known. Or he may belong to the larger number of blessed faithfuls whose names are unknown here, but treasured faithfully above. Either way, the tinging red of his life is upon the thing he did. The nations that are freest cost most in the making, in the lives of men. Every church, and every mission station, has had to use red mortar as its walls went up.

Every bit of advance ground gained for liberty and truth has been stained with the life-blood of the advance-guard. You can depend upon it that whatever you are to do that will really help must have a bit of your own self, your very life in it. Immortality of action comes only by the infusion of human blood.

Sacrifice attends us faithfully from the cradle to the body's last resting-place. The giving of one's self for others begins with the beginning of life, and never ends till life ends. Each of us comes into life through the sacrifice of the mother who bore us. That love-service of hers would not have been a sacrifice, but only a joy, had sin's cramping, restricting atmosphere not been breathed into all life. Now, with much pain, and great danger, and sometimes at the cost of life, it becomes a sacrifice. Yet it is a sacrifice of great sweet joy to her.

And that same spirit of sacrifice attends our baby years, and childhood experiences, and school-days, and times of sickness, and our matured years. The more faithfully those who make up your life-circle yield to the law of sacrifice, and give of themselves out to you, the finer and stronger you grow to be, and the sweeter life becomes to you. And every selfish shirking and shrinking back by some one impoverishes your life by so much.

A hush of awe comes over one's spirit as we recall that even for the Son of God there was no exception to this law, as He took His place down among human conditions. It was by His own blood that He saved men, and saves men. It was the spilling out of His own life that brings such blessed newness of life to us. His was a *living* sacrifice through all the years, and then greatest when that life, so long being given, was given clean out.

That sacrifice of His stands unapproached, and can never be approached by any other. His relation to sin was different from that of all other men. He made a sacrifice for men in a sense that no other can. Yet, while that is true, it is equally true that every man who follows Him will drink of His cup of sacrifice.

But it's a cup of joy now, for His drinking drained out all the bitter dregs. He asks us into the inner fellowship of His suffering. The work He began isn't yet done. He asks our help. We may fill up the measure of His sacrifice yet needed, in healing men's wounds and in throttling sin's power.

The Underground Way Into Life.

The request of the Greek pilgrims, that last tragic week, drew out of Jesus wondrous words about the law of sacrifice.[1] Their request made the necessity for His coming sacrifice stand out more sharply to His view—with edgy sharpness. The realness of that sacrifice of His stands out very vividly in the intensity of His feelings, of which we get only glimpses.

Listen to Him talking: 'if the grain of wheat doesn't suffer death, it lives; but it lives alone. But through death it may live in the midst of a harvest of golden grains. The man who turns away from the appeal of need will live a lonely life, both here and in the longer life. (Is there anything more pathetic and pitiable than selfish loneliness!) He who feels the sharp tug of need, and can't resist the appeal that calls for his life-blood, rises up through that red pathway into a blessed fellowship with the lives that owe their life to his.'

He goes on: ' he that clingeth with strong self-love to his life will find it slipping, slipping insistently out of his fingers, leaving a dry husk of a shell in his tenacious clutch. But he who in the stress of the world's emergency of need, and in the thick of the subtlest temptations to put the self-life first, treats that life as a hated enemy, to be opposed and fought, as he gives himself freely out to heal the world's hurt, *he* will find all the sweets and fragrance of life coming to him. Their unspeakable refreshment will ever increase, and never leave.'

Then follow the words that go so deep: 'if any man *would serve Me*, let him come along, putting

[1] John 12: 24–26.

his feet into my prints. Let him come through a long Nazareth life of common toil in home and shop, then along the crowded path of glad service for others, responding to every call of need. Let him come down into the shadowed olive-grove beyond Kidron's waters, up the bit of a hill outside a city wall, and deep down into the earth-soil of men's needs.

'And where I am there I will surely have that faithful follower of Mine up close by my side. He shall find himself rising up out of the common earth-life into a new life of strangely strong drawing power. And, while he will be all wrapped up in love's service, My Father will give special touches of His own hand upon his person, and upon his service.'

In one of his exquisitely quiet talks, Henry Drummond used to tell the story of a famous statue in the Fine Arts Gallery of Paris. It was the work of a great genius, who, like many a genius, was very poor, and lived in a garret which served as both studio and sleeping-room.

One midnight, when the statue was just finished, a sudden frost fell upon Paris. The sculptor lay awake in his fireless garret, and thought of the still moist clay, thought how the moisture in the pores would freeze, and the dream of his life would be destroyed in a night. So the old man rose from his cot, and wrapped his bed-clothes reverently about the statue, and lay down to his sleep.

In the morning the neighbors fond him lying dead. His life had gone out into his work. It

Ploughed up by cannon- and gun-shot, sown deep with men's lives, "worked" never so thoroughly by toiling, struggling feet, moistened with the gentle rain of dying tears, and soaked with red life, it now yields its yearly harvest of beauty. All life's a Waterloo and can be made to yield a rich growth of fragrant flowers.

The Fellowship of Scars.

And there's yet more of this winsomeness. There's a spirit power that goes out of sacrifice. It reaches far beyond the limited personal circle, out to the ends of the earth. It can't be analyzed, nor defined, nor described, but it can be felt. We don't know much about the law of spirit currents. But we know the spirit currents themselves, for every one is affected by them and every one is sending them out of himself.

You pick up a book, and suddenly find there's a something in it that takes hold of you irresistibly. A flame seems to burn in it, and then in you. Invisible fingers seem to reach out of the page and play freely up and down the key-board of your heart. Why is it? I don't know much about it. It's an elusive thing. But I can tell you my conviction, that grows stronger daily.

There's a life back of that book; there is sacrifice in that life of the keen, cutting sort; and Jesus is in that life, too, giving it His personal flavor. The life back of the book has come into the book. It's that life you are feeling as you read. Spirit power knows nothing about distance. The man who yields to sacrifice has a world-field, and is touching his field in a sense far greater than he ever knows.

And there is still more. The Master knows our sacrifices. He keenly notes the spirit that would give all, even as He did. He can breathe most of His own spirit into such a life. For it is most open to Him. He can do most through that spirit, for it comes nearest to His own. His own winsomeness breathes out of that life constantly.

There's a simple little tale that comes dressed in very homely garb. The story has in it a bit of that that makes the heart burn. It has all the marks of real life. It runs thus:

"In one poor room, that was all their home,
   A mother lay on her bed,
Her seven children around her;
   And, calling the eldest, she said:

'I'm going to leave you, Mary;
   You're nearly fourteen, you know;
And now you must be a good girl, dear,
   And make me easy to go.

'You can't depend much on father;
   But just be patient, my child,
And keep the children out of his way
   Whenever he comes home wild.

'And keep the house as well as you can;
   And, little daughter, think
He didn't use to be so;
   Remember, it's all the drink.'

The weeping daughter promised
   Always to do her best;

And, closing her eyes over weary life,
　　The mother entered her rest.

And Mary kept her promise
　　As faithfully as she might.
She cooked, and washed, and mended,
　　And kept things tidy and bright.

And when the father came home drunk,
　　The children were sent to bed,
And Mary waited alone, and took
　　The beatings in their stead.

And the little chubby fingers lost
　　Their childish softness and grace,
And toughened and chapped and calloused,
　　And the rosy, childish face

Grew thin and haggard and anxious,
　　Careworn, tired, and old,
As on those slender shoulders
　　The burdens of life were rolled.

So, when the heated season
　　Burned pitiless overhead,
And up from the filth of the noisome street
　　The fatal fever spread,

And work and want and drunken blows
　　Had weakened the tender frame,
Into the squalid room once more
　　The restful shadow came.

And Mary sent for the playmate
　　Who lived just over the way,
And said, 'The charity Doctor,
　　Has been here, Katie, to-day.

'He says I'll never be better—
　　The fever has been so bad;
And if it wasn't for one thing,
　　I'm sure I'd just be glad.

Sacrifice

'It isn't about the children;
　　I've kept my promise good,
And mother will know I stayed with them
　　As long as ever I could.

'But you know how it has been, Katie;
　　I've had so much to do,
I couldn't mind the children
　　And go to the preaching, too.

'And I've been so tired-like at night,
　　I couldn't think to pray,
And now, when I see the Lord Jesus,
　　What ever am I to say?'

And Katie, the little comforter,
　　Her help to the problem brought;
And into her heart, made wise by love,
　　The Spirit sent this thought:

'I wouldn't say a word, dear,
　　For sure He understands;
I wouldn't say ever a word at all;
　　But, Mary, *just show Him your hands!*'"

Jesus knows every scar of sacrifice you bear, and loves it. For it tells Him your love. He knows the meaning of scars, because of His own. The marks of sacrifice cement our fellowship with Him. The nearer we come to fellowship with Him in the daily touch and spirit the more freely can He reach out His own great winsomeness through us, out to His dear world.

"Won't You Save Me?"

To outsiders, who don't know about the thing, that word "sacrifice" has an ugly sound. It drives them away. But to the insiders, who have come in by the Jesus-door, there is a joyousness of the bubbling-out, singing sort, that makes the word "sacrifice," and the thing itself, clean forgot even while remembered. It is remembered as a distinct real thing, but it is pushed away from the centre of your consciousness by this song that insists on singing its music into the ears of your heart.

I said a while ago in these talks that it would be *an easy thing* for the whole Church, or even half of the Church, to take Jesus fully out to all the world. But may I tell you now plainly that it won't be an easy thing? Somebody will have to sacrifice if the thing's to be done. And that somebody will be you, if you go along where the Master calls. If you *count* on the Church doing it, or on anybody else doing it, you may be sure of one thing: some part of what needs doing won't be done.

But if you and I will reckon that this thing belongs to us, as if there were nobody else to do it, and *push on;*—well, there'll be sacrifice of the real sort and, too, there'll be all of sacrifice's peculiar winsomeness going out to draw men. And there will be men changed where you live, and out where you will never go personally.

And there will be a great joy in your heart, but with the greater joy breaking out in the Morning, when the King comes to His own.

> "I hear the sob of the parted,
> The wail of the broken-hearted,
> The sigh for the loved departed,
>   In the surging roar of the town.

Sacrifice 279

And it's, oh, for the joy of the Morning!
The light and song of the Morning!
There'll be joy in the Christmas Morning
   When the King comes to His own!

"Now let our hearts be true, brothers,
To suffer and to do, brothers;
There'll be a song for you, brothers,
   When the battle's fought and won.
It won't seem long in the Morning,
In the light and song of the Morning
There'll be joy in the Christmas Morning
   When the King comes to His own!

"Arise, and be of good cheer, brothers;
The day will soon be here, brothers;
The victory is near, brothers;
   And the sound of the glad 'Well done!'
There'll be no sad heart in the Morning
No tear will start in the Morning;
There'll be joy in the Christmas Morning
   When the King comes to His own!

"We're in for the winning side, brothers,
Bound to the Lord who died, brothers,
We shall see Him glorified, brothers,
   And the Lamb shall wear the crown.
What of the cold world's scorning?
There'll be joy enough in the Morning
There'll be joy in the Christmas Morning,
   When the King comes to His own!"

Years ago a steamer out on Lake Erie caught fire, and headed at once for the nearest land. All was wild confusion, as men and women struggled for means of escape. In the crowd was a returning California gold-miner. He fastened the belt containing his gold securely about his waist and was preparing to try to swim ashore. Just then a little sweet-faced girl in the crowd touched his hand, and looked up beseechingly into his face, and said, "Won't you please save me? I have no papa here to save me. Won't you, please?"

What would he do? He gave the belt of gold, that meant such a hard struggle, one swift glance. But that soft child-touch on his hand, and that face and voice strangely affected him. He couldn't save both;—which? The quick-as-flash thoughts came all in a heap. Then he dropped the gold, and took the child, made the plunge, and by and by reached land, utterly exhausted, and lay unconscious. As his eyes opened the child he had saved was standing over him with the tears of gratitude flooding her eyes. And a human life never seemed quite so precious. He had lost his gold, and his years of toil, but he had saved a life, and in saving it had found a new life springing up within himself.

As we close our talk together will you listen very softly. Listen: out of the distance comes a murmur of voices, like a low, long heart-cry. It comes from near-by, where you live. It comes most from far-away lands. Its words are pathetically distinct: *"Will you save me? I have no one to save me. Won't you?"* And we can do it. But the gold and the life must go. *Shall* we do it, hand in hand with Jesus, the only Saviour? Shall we *not* do it?

WITHDRAWN
from
Funderburg Library